Artificial Intelligence in Music and Audio Production

In a time when artificial intelligence (AI) is becoming increasingly integrated into music production, *Artificial Intelligence in Music and Audio Production* provides a comprehensive and easy-to-understand overview of the latest developments.

Artificial Intelligence in Music and Audio Production begins by explaining how AI is already being used in various areas of music production today, from composition and sound design to mixing, mastering, and creating music videos. Practical guides and examples show how anyone can benefit from these new technologies. Whether it's about generating synthetic vocals, transforming your own voice, or creating complete songs using text prompts—the possibilities are almost limitless. *Artificial Intelligence in Music and Audio Production* demonstrates to musicians and producers how AI can allow musicians and producers to realize their ideas faster and in more comprehensive ways, ultimately enriching their creative process.

This book will be of interest to singers, DJs, music producers, and anyone interested in the future of music—even without a deep technical background.

Thomas Foster is the founder of Foster Kent, a music production company that creates music for radio and TV stations worldwide. Notably, Foster Kent produced the music for 1010 WINS New York, which is broadcast every 20 minutes. Currently, the company is working on the new music for NewsNation, a national television network in the United States.

Artificial Intelligence in Music and Audio Production

Shaping the Sound of Tomorrow

Thomas Foster

Routledge
Taylor & Francis Group
LONDON AND NEW YORK

First published 2025
by Routledge
4 Park Square, Milton Park, Abingdon, Oxon OX14 4RN

and by Routledge
605 Third Avenue, New York, NY 10158

Routledge is an imprint of the Taylor & Francis Group, an informa business

British Library Cataloguing-in-Publication Data
A catalogue record for this book is available from the British Library

Library of Congress Cataloging-in-Publication Data
Names: Foster, Thomas (Music producer) author.
Title: Artificial intelligence in music and audio production: shaping the sound of tomorrow / Thomas Foster.
Description: [1.] | Abingdon, Oxon; New York: Routledge, 2025. | Includes bibliographical references and index.
Identifiers: LCCN 2024062006 (print) | LCCN 2024062007 (ebook) | ISBN 9781041027867 (hardback) | ISBN 9781041028338 (paperback) | ISBN 9781003621126 (ebook)
Subjects: LCSH: Artificial intelligence—Musical applications. | Sound recordings—Production and direction.
Classification: LCC ML74.3 .F67 2025 (print) | LCC ML74.3 (ebook) | DDC 780.285/63—dc23/eng/20241231
LC record available at https://lccn.loc.gov/2024062006
LC ebook record available at https://lccn.loc.gov/2024062007

ISBN: 978-1-041-02786-7 (hbk)
ISBN: 978-1-041-02833-8 (pbk)
ISBN: 978-1-003-62112-6 (ebk)

DOI: 10.4324/9781003621126

Typeset in Times New Roman
by codeMantra

Contents

Figures

Acknowledgments

First of all, I would like to express my heartfelt thanks to my subscribers. Without the constant exchange with you, your support, and your motivation, I would never have started writing a book at all—and certainly not this one. Thank you all so much! You have given my life an important new component that I wouldn't want to miss. This addition is close to music and yet an exciting new direction that brings me a lot of joy.

I also want to thank my fiancée Tatjana. A crazy person like me, who is constantly taking on new projects—be it a book, a new live show on YouTube, or another idea for a musical project—needs a partner who shares this creative madness. Tatjana, you're doing it perfectly. Thank you for being by my side and supporting me.

A very special thanks goes to my parents, who have supported me from the very beginning of my musical journey. Without you, I would never have found the courage to pursue this profession and certainly wouldn't have become such a happy person. Your support and love have paved the way for me and accompanied me at every stage.

Furthermore, I would like to thank some people with whom I have talked about artificial intelligence and who have given me important impulses for this book: Jörn Kocken, Matthias Röder, Alex Lauder, Lee Esposito, Sabine Kocher, and Tim Eller. Your input was invaluable for the creation of this book.

And lastly, I would like to thank someone who was extremely important for this book. Someone who helped me research all these topics and who perfectly corrected my poor spelling and grammar. Many thanks to the artificial intelligence.

1 The AI Revolution in Music Production

An Overview of Current Possibilities and Developments

In the summer of 2037, an aura of excitement hovers over the rooftops of Berlin. In the luxurious suite of the Adlon Hotel, the renowned super-DJ known as Sam Space and the radiant singer Joy meet to discuss final details for their upcoming performance. They sit together in the stylishly furnished living room of the suite while the city pulses beneath them in the twilight. "We should revisit the transition after the third track," says Joy thoughtfully.

Sam nods, leans back, and grins. "Watch this—I'll play you something we absolutely should include in the performance." He closes his eyes and activates his Neuralink chip to stream music from his Neural Cloud Library. Joy feels a slight buzz in her own Neuralink and receives a request: "Would you like to listen to Sam's music?" She smiles and mentally taps "Accept." Instantly, the music emerges in her mind—crystal clear, intense, and full of emotion. The neural data streams synchronize, and it's as if they both dive together into the musical world Sam has created. "This will blow people away," she says.

As they leave the room, the music suddenly stops, and the lights automatically dim. A futuristically designed limousine awaits them in front of the hotel. A glance inside reveals that no one is behind the wheel. But Sam doesn't seem bothered by this unusual situation; he casually speaks into his smartwatch: "Siri, take us to the Waldbühne Berlin."

The limousine glides silently through the streets of Berlin, while gentle yet powerful music emanates from invisible speakers. Suddenly, it's noticeable that the rhythm of the music adjusts to the unevenness of the road, as if it merges with the surroundings. This is no coincidence. An artificial intelligence adapts the music in real time to the driving situation, and Sam and Joy find themselves in the midst of a musical adventure that blurs the boundaries between reality and art.

While driving through the bustling streets of Berlin, Sam and Joy engage in lively discussion about the upcoming performance. With each passing minute, the tension rises, and the anticipation for the concert reaches its peak. Suddenly, the conversation ceases, and a pleasant silence fills the car. The artificial intelligence recognizes this quiet and begins to weave familiar vocal

DOI: 10.4324/9781003621126-1

lines into the music. The unforgettable melodies of past legends like Phil Collins and Whitney Houston blend seamlessly with the modern beats crafted by the AI.

As the limousine approaches the Waldbühne, the cheering calls of the crowd grow louder. "Sam! Sam! Sam!" echoes through the air. The two artists enter the backstage area to prepare for their performance. The energy and anticipation are palpable, and Sam can hardly wait to take the stage. To focus amid the hustle, he discreetly activates his Neuralink. Suddenly, external noises fade, and a calming silence spreads in his mind. He takes a deep breath, centers himself—ready to give it his all.

A voice from offstage announces: "Ladies and gentlemen, please welcome Sam Space!" The lights explode in a fireworks display as Sam steps up to his DJ console. Instead of traditional turntables, a futuristic control device stands before him, which he affectionately calls "The Nexus." With a smooth motion of his hands, Sam begins to conduct the music while the AI in the background generates the perfect beats and melodies.

The stage show unfolds at a new technological level: augmented reality visualizations transform the stage and surroundings in real time, as if walls and structures morph into new worlds. The interactive light show responds to the music and the movements of Joy's dance and Sam's gestures, causing beams of light and colors to dance through the space as if they were part of the performance. Simultaneously, the audience is enveloped in an immersive 360-degree sound experience. The sound doesn't just emanate from the stage but seems to come from all directions—from above, behind, and the sides—allowing the audience to fully immerse themselves in the music and visuals.

The crowd is swept away by a wave of euphoria as the bass kicks in and the stage trembles. Never before has such a combination of human passion and artificial precision been experienced. Sam controls every moment with his gestures, while Joy enchants the audience with her captivating voice.

At the end of the concert, a little boy steps backstage to ask Sam for a selfie. His eyes shine with admiration as he asks how Sam managed to build such a career. Sam smiles and replies, "It was a long journey full of creativity. I spent many years producing music with a computer." The boy looks at Sam with a gaze full of curiosity and wonder and asks, "What's a computer?"

Introduction

In 1989, the company Steinberg released the program Cubase, one of the first Digital Audio Workstations (DAWs) that allowed music to be made on a computer. This development was viewed very critically by many people at the time and was labeled as cheating. They said that only those who could play an instrument live made "real" music. Entering notes with a mouse in a piano roll seemed like trickery.

Today, we know that without this technological revolution, entire music genres like techno, hip-hop, and house wouldn't exist. Pop music would also be unthinkable without the possibilities offered by DAWs. Computer programs have revolutionized music production and made it accessible to many.

Just as DAWs did back then, artificial intelligence has made rapid advancements in recent months and years. Many people view this change critically, and that's understandable. After all, it will fundamentally change the way we make music. But I firmly believe that this development is a positive one. AI will not replace us but will open up new ways for us to be more creative and to create music that we can't even imagine today. For consumers, this means an even greater diversity and quality of music than ever before.

Similar to the introduction of DAWs, we see today that AI is redefining the role of musicians and producers. What used to be possible only through the collaboration of a large, professional team can now be realized by individuals. Artificial intelligence offers artists and producers a multitude of new tools that enable them to implement their creative vision independently and without significant costs.

Let's imagine a singer named Susanne: she never reached the point where she could produce a complete song with a program like Logic or Ableton. Nevertheless, she has a clear idea of a song she wants to create. Instead of being deterred by the technology, she simply opens her ChatGPT app and starts talking about her feelings and emotions. Through dialogue with the AI, song lyrics develop that exactly match her ideas—something she might never have achieved on her own, especially not in a foreign language like English.

But that's just the beginning. With her finished text, Susanne goes to the website SUNO, an AI-based platform for music generation. There, she copies her song lyrics into a designated field and also provides a detailed text prompt that describes how the song should sound—the desired mood, genre, instrumentation, and type of vocals. SUNO then delivers the first suggestions for fully produced songs that already include a realistic-sounding vocal track. Not entirely satisfied with the initial results, she further optimizes her text prompt, refines her descriptions, and adjusts details until she's completely happy with the final song.

Subsequently, Susanne downloads the so-called stems—the individual tracks of the song, such as drums, bass, other instruments, and vocals. She opens Logic Pro and imports these stems to record her own vocal tracks and further refine the production. To optimally integrate her voice into the mix and enhance the sound, she uses the tool Neutron 5 from the company iZotope, which utilizes artificial intelligence to analyze the vocals and automatically process them to achieve professional quality. After perfecting the vocals, Susanne uploads the finished song to the website LANDR.com to perform the mastering. LANDR offers an AI-based solution to adjust the overall sound of the song so that it stands out alongside other current productions on platforms like Spotify. What previously would have required the collaboration of at least four specialized professionals and high costs, Susanne now achieves alone—supported by artificial intelligence.

Thanks to these technologies, she can produce a song that perfectly reflects her feelings and artistic vision without the hurdles previously associated with music production. She feels the song is 100% her own, even though she used AI assistance in areas that aren't her strengths. For the listener, ultimately, only the emotional experience the music conveys matters—regardless of whether the production was supported by humans or machines. Today, AI also enables DJs to produce songs without external singers or allows producers to create music without expensive studios or external help. The democratization of music production continues to advance, offering everyone the opportunity to express their creativity freely.

However fascinating and enriching these new possibilities may be for us musicians, there are developments that are equally concerning and dramatic for our future. According to a global study commissioned by the International Confederation of Societies of Authors and Composers (Cisac), creators of music and audiovisual content could lose about a quarter of their income by 2028, primarily due to the growing prevalence of generative AI applications.

This prediction is alarming and raises many questions. What does it mean for the future of musicians when the value of creative work is increasingly undermined by machine-generated content? How can we, as artists, continue to thrive in such an environment?

Nevertheless, in this book, I want to focus on the positive aspects: the opportunities these technologies provide us as music creators to become even more creative, to develop our unique styles, and to make our music accessible to a wider audience.

As Jacob Collier insightfully put it, "AI as a tool in music-making is fine, but it's always going to be the humanity in music that makes people want to listen to it." This sentiment highlights an important truth: while we cannot change the course of technological development, we can decide how to use it to our advantage. Ultimately, it is the humanity, the emotions, and the personal touch in music that will always set us apart from machines—and deeply resonate with listeners.

How Does Artificial Intelligence Work in the Field of Music?

Artificial Intelligence (AI) and its subfields—Machine Learning (ML) and Deep Learning (DL)—have fundamentally transformed the way music is produced and composed. But what exactly is going on beneath the surface? Simply put, AI learns from data, much like a musician who improves by listening and practicing. In machine learning, a trainable computer model is fed large amounts of musical data—such as songs, chords, melodies, or even entire productions. This model identifies patterns within the data and uses interconnected virtual "neurons" to generate music or offer suggestions.

Neural Networks and Their Structure

A particularly effective form of machine learning is deep learning, which uses what are known as artificial neural networks. These networks resemble the structure of the human brain and consist of multiple layers of "neurons." Think of these neurons as simple decision units that do more than just return a binary answer ("0" or "1"). Instead, they output values between 0 and 1, representing probabilities. For example, if the question is, "Does this image contain a flower?" the network does not respond with a definite "yes" or "no," but might give a probability like 0.567. This number indicates a 56.7% chance that a flower is present. Based on a predefined threshold (e.g., 0.5), the result can then be interpreted as "yes." The network itself, however, never returns a hard "0" or "1," but rather a spectrum of values derived from recognized patterns and their assigned weights.

These neurons are arranged in different layers, as illustrated below:

- Input Layer: This layer receives the raw data, such as the pixels of an image or the frequencies of a music sample. Each neuron in this layer passes the information on to the next layer.
- Hidden Layers: These layers further process the information by searching for specific patterns, such as certain timbres or chord progressions. Each layer learns to perform a specific task, enabling the network to recognize increasingly complex features.
- Output Layer: This layer produces the final result, for example, the probability that a music track belongs to a certain genre or which chords should be played next (Figure 1.1).

The more layers a neural network has, the more complex the patterns it can detect, and the more nuanced its decisions become. In the musical domain, this enables AI to identify sound patterns, compose new melodies, or suggest harmonies that complement a particular composition's style.

How AI Generates Music

The development of such an AI system begins with developers training it using large datasets—thousands of songs from various genres, for instance. During this training process, the AI learns which combinations of notes, harmonies, and rhythms fit well together, or what a particular genre typically sounds like. Once properly trained, the AI can be applied in various ways: as

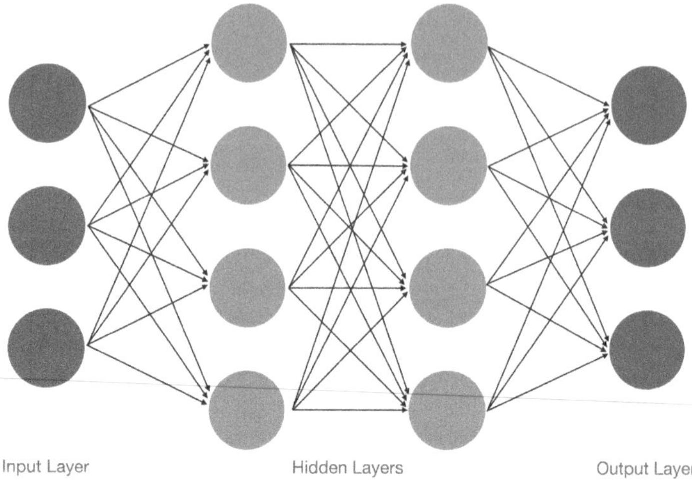

Figure 1.1 Neural Networks Consisting of an Input Layer, Hidden Layers, and an Output Layer.

an assistant suggesting melodies or harmonies, as a composer creating entire pieces of music, or even as a producer optimizing a track's sound mix.

It's important to note, however, that AI is not "creative" in the human sense. It works with probabilities and patterns gleaned from the data it has studied, recombining them in novel ways. True creativity emerges when humans use these tools to bring their musical vision to life and explore new forms of expression. Much like the advent of Digital Audio Workstations (DAWs), the use of AI in music production represents a new level of democratization, where technological tools help artists realize their creative ideas more easily and rapidly.

2 Legal Issues Surrounding AI Music

An Overview of Copyright, Licensing, and More

The rapid development of artificial intelligence opens up new creative horizons but also raises a variety of legal questions. Can the works created using AI be claimed as one's intellectual property? What potential challenges could arise, and what aspects should be considered? These questions form the core of this chapter, where I attempt to bring clarity to a complex topic.

Although I am not a lawyer, I have gained more experience in dealing with legal issues in the music industry throughout my career than I might have preferred. To provide a well-founded insight, I invited a renowned lawyer from Munich, Tim Eller, to my podcast "Thomas Foster Music Production." Tim has a profound understanding of the legal challenges associated with artificial intelligence and discussed possible solutions in our conversation. He also kindly reviewed, corrected, and expanded the manuscript for this chapter.

To understand how the music industry works and which rights are relevant here, I want to start with a little story:

Our story begins with a lyricist who has written a text. Let's call him Shakespeare. Shakespeare is very enthusiastic about his text and wants to turn it into a song. So, he goes to his neighbor, whom we'll call Beethoven, and asks if he can compose a melody for his text. Beethoven writes a melody, and both register the resulting song with their respective performing rights organizations. In Germany, this would be GEMA; in the United States, it would be ASCAP or BMI, and in the United Kingdom, PRS for Music. These organizations register the title, the date, as well as Shakespeare as the lyricist and Beethoven as the composer.

However, there is an important difference between the two: Beethoven decides to assign his rights to a publisher, while Shakespeare does not. In the past, the publisher was responsible for printing sheet music; today, they manage the exploitation of copyrights and sometimes even promote the song. For this, the publisher receives about 30%–40% of the revenue Beethoven earns with this composition. Shakespeare, on the other hand, must take care of the exploitation himself but retains 100% of the revenue he receives from the rights organization (such as GEMA, ASCAP, PRS for Music, etc.).

DOI: 10.4324/9781003621126-2

Now, Shakespeare and Beethoven want their song to be recorded. So, they go to a mutual friend, whom we'll call Quincy. Quincy is a music producer and is very enthusiastic about the song. So, he immediately calls his favorite singer, whom we'll call Whitney. When Whitney arrives at the studio a little later, Quincy has already produced a playback on which Whitney sings the song. The hit is ready.

To release this song, Quincy turns to a record label and signs a contract for the exploitation of the song. The label receives all the rights to release this song and usually gives about 50% of all revenue to Quincy. The label then uploads the song through a digital distributor to platforms like Spotify, Apple Music, and all other streaming services. However, the song does not appear immediately but only after a few weeks, giving Quincy, Whitney, and the label enough time to promote their song in advance. Additionally, all three parties can pitch the song to Spotify and other streaming platforms, which means filling out an online form to increase their chances of being included in playlists and thus gaining more attention.

Their song becomes a big hit and is played all over the world. Using the "Spotify for Artists" app, Quincy, Whitney, and the label can track exactly which playlists the song lands on, in which countries, and how often it is played.

The streaming platforms pay fees to performing rights organizations like GEMA, ASCAP, or PRS for Music for the rights to the musical works (lyrics and composition) that are played on their platform. These fees are paid as compensation for copyrights or authors' rights. The platforms also provide information about the use of the songs, including the number of plays, to the rights organizations. These organizations retain about 15%–20% of the revenue as administrative costs and distribute the rest to their members according to a fixed distribution key.

The rights organizations distribute the money according to their distribution key and pay it out to the authors. Shakespeare gets 50% of the authors' rights, Beethoven's publisher receives 15%–30%, and the rest goes to Beethoven.

Additionally, Spotify pays directly to the distributor for the neighboring rights. The distributor retains a certain percentage of these revenues depending on the contract and passes the rest on to the label. The label then pays the agreed 50% of these revenues to Quincy, the producer. Quincy, in turn, gives an agreed percentage of his earnings to Whitney.

Since the song is a big hit, it is also played on the radio. Radio stations, in turn, pay the rights organizations for the copyrights and the organizations for neighboring rights, such as GVL in Germany or SoundExchange in the United States. The rights organizations also distribute these amounts to the authors, while the neighboring rights organizations pay the record label and all participating singers and musicians, such as Quincy and Whitney.

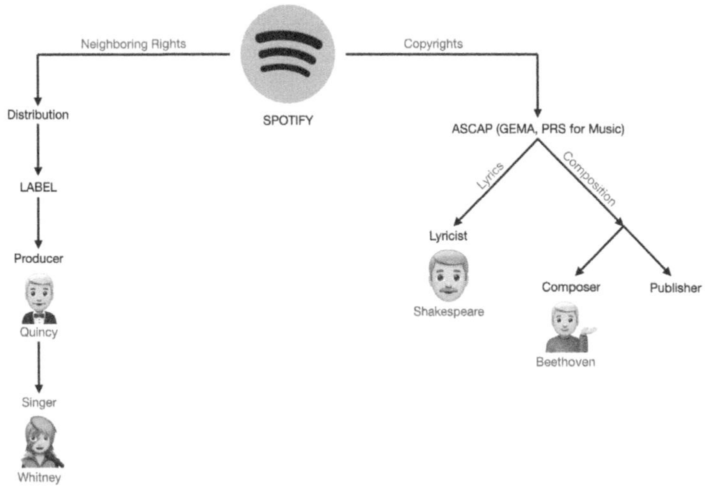

Figure 2.1 Revenue Distribution on Spotify

To summarize, there are two ways to earn money:

- Copyrights: Through performing rights organizations like GEMA, ASCAP, or PRS for Music, lyricists, composers, and potential publishers earn money.
- Neighboring Rights: Through the record label and organizations like GVL or SoundExchange, producers, singers, and all involved musicians earn money from streaming revenues and broadcasts on radio, TV, and events (Figure 2.1).

Changes in the Music Industry in General

The traditional role distribution in the modern music industry has already seen significant changes before the age of AI. Today, there are many independent artists in the music industry who take on multiple roles in the production of their musical works. They act as singers, producers, composers, lyricists, and are often their own record label. This development is often referred to as "DIY" (Do-It-Yourself) or "independent" because the artists want to retain control over all aspects of their music.

Through digital distribution platforms like DistroKid or LANDR, these artists can independently and directly upload their music to streaming platforms without signing a traditional record contract. This allows artists to release their music faster and more independently and to benefit directly from the revenues without a record label or rights organization acting as an intermediary.

This development has greatly changed the music industry but has also opened up new opportunities for many artists to make their music accessible to a global audience. It is an exciting trend that shows how the industry is evolving and how artists are increasingly taking control of their own music.

In Austria, the collecting society for music copyrights and related rights is managed by AKM. In Switzerland, the corresponding society is SUISA (Société Suisse des Auteurs, Compositeurs et Editeurs de Musique). In the United States, there are several, including ASCAP and BMI, while in the United Kingdom, PRS for Music manages the rights.

Changes in the Music Industry Due to AI

The most significant and not yet fully foreseeable changes are likely to come from artificial intelligence (AI). This raises many interesting factual and legal questions, offering both uncertainty and opportunities.

Can I Claim a Song Lyric Written by ChatGPT as My Own?

In our example, Shakespeare discovers an AI application called ChatGPT. With the help of ChatGPT, text instructions (so-called prompts) can be formulated in an input field. Shakespeare creates such a prompt that reads, "Write me lyrics for a pop ballad on the theme of love!" The result is astonishing, and Shakespeare is delighted with the outcome. The result is a complete and high-quality song lyric. However, he wonders whether he can claim this text as his own and register the song as the lyricist with a performing rights organization like GEMA (Germany), ASCAP (USA), PRS for Music (UK), or a similar organization.

The starting point of copyright law and the unique aspects surrounding AI present us with many unresolved issues. For instance, in many countries like Germany, the basis is the concept of a "work" under copyright law. According to the German Copyright Act, only "personal intellectual creations" qualify as protected works. Based on this deeply rooted principle of originality, a human creator is required for a work to be protected. In the past, there was consensus that a self-portrait of a monkey (like Naruto's "Monkey Selfie") or a picture painted by an elephant with its trunk could not be granted copyright protection.

There have already been attempts in the past to create works, such as images, using algorithms or AI (e.g., "Edmond de Belamy" or "The Next Rembrandt" project). These projects led to heated debates about whether these AI-generated works could be protected by copyright. These cases were mostly theoretical, not practical. However, the situation changed dramatically when AI became a mass phenomenon with significant economic impact. As a result, these essentially not entirely new questions have been increasingly hotly debated, especially since the success of applications like ChatGPT.

In our case, Shakespeare now wonders whether he holds the copyright for the text generated with the help of ChatGPT. When I asked ChatGPT, the AI confirmed the authorship. However, lawyer Tim Eller provides some necessary caution and explains the complexities of this topic.

Tim states that questions around AI are still largely unresolved from a legal perspective. We are, at best, in a gray area, and there are often no clear regulations. While the European Union recently passed the so-called "AI Act," the world's first comprehensive regulatory framework for AI, it primarily addresses questions about the permissibility of various AI solutions. However, it leaves questions about copyright largely unanswered.

Given the current situation, the general rules of copyright law must be applied. Therefore, the question arises whether the music piece created by Shakespeare with the help of ChatGPT can be considered a "work" under copyright law. According to Tim, it might already lack the necessary personal intellectual creation by Shakespeare.

To qualify as a creation under copyright law, it is necessary to reach a certain threshold known as "sufficient originality." The requirements for this are relatively low. A relatively minor individual creative contribution can be sufficient to meet the originality threshold (known as the "small change" principle).

In the past, even short texts like SMS messages with up to 140 characters have been subject to legal debates on this topic. Due to the brevity of SMS messages, special circumstances must be present for copyright protection to apply based on individualization in exceptional cases. The shorter a text, the more it must creatively stand out from common texts. According to Tim, these principles can largely be applied to prompts given to AI systems. The shorter and simpler a prompt, the less likely it is to qualify for copyright protection. Furthermore, Tim argues that there should be a distinction between the copyright protection of the prompt itself and the output, i.e., the supposed "work" generated by the AI. Even if Shakespeare could possibly claim copyright protection for the prompt, this would not necessarily mean he could also claim it for the text generated by the AI.

Based on this information, Shakespeare decides to write a new text and not just use a single short prompt. He wants to work closely with ChatGPT, using the AI tool as a "partner" in an ongoing creative process. First, he writes an initial prompt and explains to the machine what the text should be about. ChatGPT offers several suggestions for the song title or hook. Shakespeare chooses one. Through a longer process involving many intermediate steps and new prompts, a text is created in collaboration between human and machine. The machine is merely used as a tool. Now, Shakespeare has no reservations about considering this text his intellectual property and registering it under his name with a rights organization like GEMA, ASCAP, or PRS for Music. A final determination of whether the result can enjoy copyright protection and whether the use is in line with the terms of service of the AI provider can only be made on a case-by-case basis. Significant legal uncertainties and risks remain under current circumstances.

Therefore, it is always essential to check the specific terms of use for each AI tool. In the case of ChatGPT, OpenAI generally transfers the usage rights of the content generated by ChatGPT to the user who made the request. This means you have the right to use, modify, and distribute the texts generated by ChatGPT.

Could a Song Created with ChatGPT Infringe Existing Copyrights?

An artificial intelligence is always trained on large amounts of data (training datasets), which generally include existing works. In the case of ChatGPT, this consists of many books, articles, and even numerous existing song lyrics. It becomes problematic if the training dataset includes copyrighted works without proper authorization. It is impossible to completely rule out that newly generated texts might contain phrases or even lines from existing songs, potentially infringing on existing copyrights.

The same issue can, in fact, happen to humans: we might write a few lines of text or come up with a beautiful melody spontaneously, only to realize later that it already exists. In the case of texts, this can fortunately be easily checked by entering the relevant lines into a search engine like Google. However, this process is naturally more complex for music and images.

A recent example from the visual arts industry highlights the problem: Getty Images, one of the largest providers of image and photo libraries, has sued Stability AI. Stability AI is working on artificial intelligence that generates images and has used millions of images to train its AI. Getty Images accuses them of using their images without consent. This case is still ongoing and could last several years. The outcome of the lawsuit could have far-reaching implications for the AI industry, particularly for the development and use of generative models.

Can I Upload a Song Created with SUNO or UDIO to Spotify?

To find out, I took a closer look at the terms of use of UDIO:

According to Section 6.3 of the terms of service, the content you create belongs to you. The company does not claim ownership rights to your content, except for the rights to the software and technology used to generate the output. You may use your output songs for both personal and commercial purposes as long as you comply with the terms of use. The company grants you the right to download a copy of your output songs, consisting of an audio file, for such purposes.

The terms also include provisions on attribution. If you use your output songs or content publicly, you must indicate that the output was generated with UDIO's services. However, if you subscribe to the paid services, this requirement does not apply to output generated during your subscription.

However, it may be challenging to register such a song with a performing rights organization like GEMA (Germany), ASCAP (USA), or PRS for Music (UK) under your own name. This is because it is clear that, with a song generated by UDIO, you likely did not make a creative contribution and therefore do not have a legitimate copyright claim.

Summary: You can upload a song created with UDIO or SUNO to Spotify and other streaming services. It is recommended to use the paid version of SUNO or UDIO. However, it is not appropriate to register this song with a performing rights organization like GEMA, ASCAP, or BMI. Instead, you could enter "Generated with UDIO" or "Generated with SUNO" in the fields for lyrics and composition.

This version now includes references to various performing rights organizations (GEMA, ASCAP, PRS for Music, BMI) to ensure the text is relevant and accessible to an international audience.

Can I Release a Song with an AI Voice That Sounds Like Madonna?

First of all, many users have used websites like Lalals.com to transform their singing into the voice of a famous star and have released these songs without facing any problems. I, too, have released an ABBA song featuring the voices of Ed Sheeran, Britney Spears, Madonna, and many others.

Thomas Foster—Money—on Spotify:

https://open.spotify.com/track/2v6Da7UMX7EHLCe4dqkScv?si=e56b3d8878134f87

There seems to be an unwritten rule in the music industry: if you release a song that gets less than a million plays, it is unlikely that you will face legal consequences for potential infringements. Record labels generally only pay attention to highly successful tracks, which is why it is advisable to be aware of potential risks beforehand. Since the future is unpredictable and you can't always foresee if a song will go viral, let's take a closer look at the situation:

Lalals claims that their service is legal because they ensure their AI voices are trained exclusively with legal material and encourage their users to use a celebrity's voice without claiming it is the actual voice of the celebrity. Although a Lalals employee stated in a podcast that this is legal because they only say "Ed Sheeran-inspired" and do not claim it is actually Ed Sheeran, legal expert Tim Eller raises concerns about potential violations of copyright and personality rights.

Lalals explains it as follows:

"Yes, we ensure that our service is compliant and legal, and our AI voices are only trained with legal material. You can also release your song if you use a celebrity's voice, which is completely legal under copyright law—but it is recommended not to state that the actual celebrity is heard on this song." In my podcast, a Lalals employee explained that their service is legal because they say "Ed Sheeran-inspired" and do not claim that it is Ed Sheeran.

However, this statement is viewed critically by legal experts like Tim Eller, as he sees potential violations of copyright and personality rights. Therefore, it would be wise to be cautious when releasing songs using such voices.

Lalals, Audimee, and other platforms offer many voices that sound great without trying to mimic a famous star. Using these voices should be unproblematic.

Regulation of AI in Music: Consequences and Perspectives

In March 2024, the European Parliament passed the EU law on the regulation of artificial intelligence, known as the EU AI Act. In Europe, an important aspect of this law, which is particularly relevant for AI and music, is the requirement to label AI-generated content. This regulation will come into effect in 2026. This means that streaming platforms like Spotify in Europe will be required to label songs that are generated using artificial intelligence. Here are some considerations regarding the potential impact of this regulation in Europe:

- Playlist Curators: Individuals or companies that create playlists for Spotify in Europe may avoid AI-labeled songs, as they may consider songs generated by humans to be more musically valuable.
- Algorithmic Preference: The algorithms and playlists of Spotify, YouTube, and other streaming platforms currently determine which music becomes successful and which does not. In Europe, streaming platforms may tend to promote AI-generated music less than music created by humans.
- In-House AI Music Production by Spotify: In Europe, there are frequent rumors that Spotify could produce music with AI itself to pay less to record labels and rights organizations such as GEMA. However, no evidence has been provided for this so far.

At this point, it is difficult to predict how the music industry in Europe will change due to this law. However, it is believed that any form of transparency, including a labeling requirement, is likely to improve the situation.

Situation Outside Europe

In the United States, there is currently no specific requirement to label AI-generated music on streaming platforms like Spotify. Similarly, in the United Kingdom, the regulation of AI in music is less strict, although these markets are also grappling with issues related to copyright and the use of AI in creative processes. In many other parts of the world, such as Asia, regulation is even less clearly defined, and there is currently no unified approach to labeling AI-generated content. However, the legal situation may change rapidly as governments worldwide increasingly examine the impact of AI on various industries.

Legal Dispute Over AI Music Training

At the end of June 2024, major music labels Warner Music Group, Sony Music Entertainment, and Universal Music Group filed a lawsuit against AI music companies Suno and UDIO. They allege that Suno and UDIO used copyrighted music to train their AI without obtaining the necessary licenses. The affected artists include prominent names such as Billie Eilish, Jon Bon Jovi, and Nicki Minaj.

Initially, Suno and UDIO referred to the principle of "fair use" and argued that the use of music to train their AI was legally permissible. However, in early August 2024, they admitted that they had indeed used copyrighted recordings of artists without the proper licenses. This is a significant concession that the companies made only under the pressure of the lawsuit. The record companies claim that this admission proves that Suno and UDIO unlawfully copied material to train their AI models.

If the labels are successful, it could lead other AI developers to take stricter measures to ensure they acquire the necessary licenses to train their models. Additionally, AI companies may be forced to adjust their business models to avoid legal conflicts. Established music labels could further consolidate their market share, while new AI-based providers might face greater hurdles to enter the market. Overall, the lawsuit against Suno and UDIO could significantly affect the dynamics of the music industry and pave the way for future regulations and standards in dealing with AI and copyrighted material.

GEMA Sues OpenAI

A Precedent in the Intersection of AI and Copyright Law

The increasing integration of artificial intelligence (AI) in creative processes has not only opened new possibilities but also introduced legal and ethical challenges. A prominent example is the lawsuit filed by GEMA, Germany's performance rights organization comparable to ASCAP in the United States and PRS for Music in the United Kingdom, against OpenAI, the developer of the AI-based chatbot ChatGPT. This is the first lawsuit of its kind in Europe, specifically targeting the unlicensed use of copyrighted song lyrics by an AI platform.

Background of the Lawsuit

On November 13, 2024, GEMA filed a lawsuit against OpenAI in the Munich Regional Court. The organization alleges that OpenAI used copyrighted song lyrics from GEMA members without obtaining the necessary licenses. The lawsuit targets both OpenAI's European subsidiary in Ireland and its parent company in the United States.

According to GEMA, the song lyrics were systematically used to train the AI models behind ChatGPT. Tobias Holzmüller, Managing Director of GEMA, stated:

> Our members' songs are not free raw material for the business models of providers of generative AI systems. Anyone who wants to use these songs must obtain a license and fairly compensate the authors.

GEMA emphasizes that other providers, such as Genius or Musixmatch, pay licensing fees for the use of song lyrics, whereas OpenAI has allegedly consciously refrained from doing so. The lawsuit is thus an attempt to enforce the rights of approximately 95,000 GEMA members.

The Legal Basis

OpenAI defends itself by invoking the US principle of "Fair Use," which under certain circumstances allows the use of copyrighted works without a license. In Europe, however, stricter regulations apply, and GEMA argues that using song lyrics to train an AI does not fall under "Fair Use." Instead, it constitutes systematic copyright infringement.

A central point of the lawsuit is the reproduction of protected song lyrics by the AI when users request them. GEMA contends that this not only violates the rights of the authors but also undermines the value of their creative work.

Implications for the Creative Industry

The GEMA lawsuit exemplifies the challenges that AI brings to the creative industry. While the technology offers enormous potential to analyze, generate, or personalize music, it also conflicts with the rights of creators.

Should the lawsuit be decided in favor of GEMA, it could serve as a precedent and lay the foundation for stricter regulation in dealing with AI and copyrighted material. It would send a strong signal to other companies that the use of creative works for AI systems has clear boundaries.

Conclusion

The lawsuit by GEMA against OpenAI marks a turning point in handling copyrighted material by AI. It highlights the importance of establishing clear regulations that enable technological advancement without violating the rights of creators. For the music industry and the AI sector, it remains to be seen how this case will unfold—and what lessons will be learned from it.

Artificial Intelligence Meets Music

How GEMA Ensures Fair Compensation

In September 2024, GEMA—the German performance rights organization similar to ASCAP in the United States and PRS for Music in the United Kingdom—became the first collective management organization worldwide to introduce a licensing model for generative artificial intelligence (AI). This model aims to ensure that musicians are fairly compensated for the use of their works in training AI systems and in the creation of new AI-generated music.

Why Is AI in Music a Concern?

Generative AI can create new music pieces by learning from existing, copyrighted works. Training such AI models with protected music is an intensive form of usage, as it relies on the creative output of the original artists. Therefore, it's crucial that these artists are appropriately compensated when their works are used for such purposes.

The Two-Pillar Licensing Model of GEMA

GEMA has developed a licensing framework based on two main components:

1 Licensing of AI Providers

- Revenue Sharing: Providers of AI systems trained with copyrighted music are required to allocate 30% of their net revenues to the authors. This includes income from subscriptions, licenses, and other revenue streams directly related to the AI-generated output.

- Minimum Compensation: Even if minimal or no profits are made, a minimum compensation is stipulated. This is based on the volume of AI-generated music and ensures that artists are always fairly remunerated.

2 Licensing of Subsequent Uses

- Legal Certainty for Users: Individuals or companies wishing to use and monetize AI-generated music—such as background tracks or content on streaming platforms—must obtain a license. This protects them from potential copyright infringements.
- Involvement of the Authors: The original artists are included in the revenue from these subsequent uses. The compensation should be at least equivalent to what it would have been for using human-created music.

Benefits of the Model

- For Artists: They receive fair compensation for the use of their works in AI systems and for new music generated from them.
- For AI Providers and Users: They benefit from clear licensing conditions and legal certainty, promoting innovation and creative applications.
- For the Market: A fair balance is established between technological advancement and the protection of creative achievements.

Conclusion

With this licensing model, GEMA takes a significant step toward protecting the rights of music creators in the age of artificial intelligence. It fosters technological progress without neglecting the creative contributions of authors. This ensures that music—whether generated by humans or machines—continues to be valued and fairly compensated. Special thanks to Tim Eller for his assistance with this chapter.

3 SUNO & UDIO

The Future of Music Production? A Look at the Groundbreaking AI Tool for Creating Complete Songs

Introduction: The Discovery at the Airport

In early 2024, I found myself at Munich Airport with my business partner Peter and a friend from New York. We were on our way to Cologne to visit friends who work at a radio station there. It was one of those typically hectic airport moments: people hurried by, announcements echoed through the halls, and I tried to make meaningful use of the last few minutes before boarding. As I scrolled through my smartphone, a message caught my eye that immediately electrified me: a new web platform called Suno could generate music of unprecedented quality solely from a text prompt.

Suno promised a revolutionary way of music production, fundamentally different from previous attempts to create music using artificial intelligence (AI). Curiosity grabbed me, and without hesitation, I opened the Suno website, signed up, and began to explore what this new platform had to offer.

First Experiences with Suno

I quickly realized that Suno allows you to generate music by entering a simple text prompt describing how the song should sound. But there was also an advanced option: by toggling the "Custom" switch, you could set additional criteria, including entering your own song lyrics. I was eager to try this flexibility and chose this second option. Spontaneously, I opened my ChatGPT app to create song lyrics that reflected our connection to our friends in Cologne.

I told ChatGPT about our experiences with Jonas and Markus, two longtime friends, and recalled the last time we were their guests. An especially unforgettable moment was when I went to the bathroom and found the bathtub already filled—strewn with rose petals, an extraordinary gesture of hospitality. I also shared how much we looked forward to this return visit, the beautiful evening that awaited us, and experiencing that warm hospitality again. Within seconds, ChatGPT provided me with lyrics that perfectly captured all these emotions.

DOI: 10.4324/9781003621126-3

The Magic of AI: Song Creation in Real-Time

With the finished song lyrics prepared, I activated the "Custom" switch in Suno to use the advanced options and insert my own text. I also specified that I wanted an emotional, danceable song—a mix of deep, soulful melodies and a driving beat. Barely a minute later, the first two versions of the song were ready. Full of excitement, I started the first version and listened.

What happened next was a moment that showed me the possibilities of the future: the song began with an atmospheric intro, featuring a Fender Rhodes playing chords that immediately reminded me of the timeless harmonies of a Stevie Wonder or Whitney Houston song. After the short intro, powerful male vocals set in—his timbre and the way he blended into the mix instantly brought to mind the big hits of the Swedish House Mafia. Accompanying this was a deep house groove that exuded an intense, captivating energy.

Here we are again, heading to Cologne,
Remembering the last time, when love was shown.
Jonas and Markus, our hearts are moved,
Roses in the bathtub, emotions soothed.

Suddenly, the groove stopped, and the singer switched to a higher octave. At that moment, his voice gained even more power and presence, as if it filled the entire acoustic space and reached an intensity that was hard to believe. The production sounded so flawless, as if it had been crafted by one of the top American producers, with all the subtleties and refinements that make an international production stand out.

The vocals were "doubled"—a technique where multiple takes of the same vocal track are layered to create a wide and full sound. These additional voices were mixed far left and right in the stereo field, making the vocals incredibly present and wide. Effects like delay and exciter, which provided additional depth and brilliance, were perfectly set. The compression and EQ were also top-notch, allowing the vocals to effortlessly hold their own against the driving beat.

The chorus hit me right in the heart. The melody was incredibly beautiful and emotional, carried by harmonies that were simply perfect. The names of our hosts were highlighted, giving the chorus a personal touch that made the song something truly special.

Jonas and Markus,
You set the bar high,
With roses and love,
You touched the sky.

Your warm invitation,
So heartfelt and clear,

We can't wait for the evening
With friends so dear.

Was the Sound Perfect?

Was the sound perfect? No, it wasn't 100% flawless. There was a slight limitation in quality that I recognized from previous projects involving artificial intelligence. The highs were somewhat reduced, and there were very slight artifacts. I would describe it as a sound reminiscent of a not-quite-perfect MP3. But compared to past projects, it was so subtle that most people wouldn't notice it on standard speakers. If this song played on a car radio or an Alexa device, no one would suspect that it wasn't a high-quality production but was created using artificial intelligence. Only on headphones or studio monitors could you detect this slight limitation.

A Magical Evening in Cologne

A few hours later, we arrived at our friends' place in Cologne. They enthusiastically showed us their new apartment and the accompanying fantastic Tuscan garden—something I had never seen with an apartment in Germany before. After dinner, as we opened the second bottle of wine, I told my friends I had a surprise for them. I sent them the audio file of the song and asked them to play it loudly on their system.

When the chorus played, both of them jumped up and embraced me and my friends. We all felt the emotions of this song, which celebrated our friendship and turned this wonderful evening into an especially magical moment.

The Aftermath: From YouTube to a TV Documentary

Two days later, back in my studio in Salzburg, I produced a video for my YouTube channel demonstrating Suno's functionality. I titled the video "Suno—AI Produces Music—I'm Unemployed!!!". In the video, you see me creating a text prompt with Suno to craft a song, and you hear my voice as I listen to the result. After the first lines, I say, "Okay, that sounds exciting," and during the chorus of this newly generated song, I exclaim emotionally, "Oh my God, I'm unemployed!"

This video quickly went viral, reaching over 100,000 views on YouTube in a short time. The attention did not go unnoticed: the TV channel 3Sat became aware of me and invited me to be the main protagonist in their documentary "Artificial Music—The AI Revolution in Pop."

Closing Words: The New Era of Creativity

This experience with Suno showed me that we are on the cusp of a new era in music production—a time when artificial intelligence not only serves as a tool for generating sounds but can act as a true creative partner. The emotions this song generated in just a few minutes were so authentic and powerful that I have no doubt: we are witnessing the beginning of a new revolution.

A Deeper Look into Suno's Capabilities

In the weeks following my first experiment with Suno, I couldn't let go and delved deeper into the possibilities these AI-based platforms offer. I wanted to understand where their strengths lie and where their weaknesses become apparent. What I quickly noticed was that Suno is a fantastic composer. And as hard as it is for me to admit, Suno is definitely a better composer than I am. But that's hardly surprising; in a way, it feels as if the combined experience of musical greats like Mozart, John Lennon, Michael Jackson, Prince, and Bruno Mars—and many more—flows into every song.

I was particularly impressed by Suno's ability to perfectly reproduce older music styles from the '80s or the early 2000s. The harmonic structures, instrumentations, and even the characteristic sound aesthetics of these eras are replicated with such quality that it often made me pause. It was almost as if you were transported into a music studio from those times.

However, the more I tested Suno, the more a weakness became apparent: when it came to current music styles dominating the charts—be it hyper techno or other genres of electronic music—I hit clear limits. Even if the sound quality were flawless, completely perfect, Suno couldn't deliver the fresh, innovative sound that a modern label would be looking for. A dance track that could compete in today's charts likely wouldn't emerge this way.

The Limits of Artificial Intelligence

This observation led me to a fundamental question: Is it only a matter of time before Suno also learns this modern musical language? Could it happen that an AI one day not only reproduces but also innovates? To better understand this topic, I engaged in numerous conversations with other musicians, producers, and especially with experts deeply involved in programming and training artificial intelligence.

One aspect repeatedly emphasized in these discussions was: Artificial intelligence can perfectly learn and replicate existing things. It is essentially designed to recognize patterns in vast amounts of data and reproduce them—and over time, it will probably do this better than we humans. After all, we cannot learn infinitely; we have only a limited lifetime to absorb and process a certain amount of musical styles and techniques. An AI like Suno, however, can access endless databases, achieving impressive diversity and precision.

But what an AI cannot do is truly advance music. It lacks creative curiosity, the ability for self-evaluation, and an instinctive understanding of what moves people emotionally. Suno cannot independently come up with the idea to try something entirely new, something that has never been attempted before. It cannot listen to itself, critically consider why it's not yet perfect, and adjust it until something new emerges that everyone who hears it thinks, "Wow, that's new!"

The Essence of Musical Innovation

Indeed, when we look at many of the songs that have become big international hits, a crucial factor was often precisely that: these songs did something no one had done before. They pushed music a bit further, often through a mix of technical innovation, emotional depth, and cultural relevance. From The Beatles to modern artists like Billie Eilish or Kanye West—they all, in their own way, have pushed musical boundaries and redefined audience expectations.

While Suno is capable of composing impressive music and perfectly replicating a remarkable range of styles, the creative leap that leads to true innovation remains a deeply human ability. It's the human element of creativity—the unpredictable, the imperfect, the struggle and search for that unique sound no one has heard before—that ultimately distinguishes us as artists.

As David Guetta observed, AI undoubtedly represents the future of music, but it should be seen "as a tool." The question we face in this new era of AI and music production isn't whether AI can replace us as musicians. Rather, it's: How can we use these technologies to expand our own creativity? How can we, in collaboration between human and machine, create new musical worlds that inspire us as artists and listeners alike? These considerations will be crucial for the sound of the future—and perhaps it's precisely this combination of human intuition and technological precision that will lead us there.

SUNO: Artificial Intelligence for Music Creation

SUNO is an innovative platform that impressively demonstrates the possibilities of artificial intelligence in music production. To use SUNO, you visit the homepage suno.com and create an account. After a successful login, you reach the main page, which offers a clear and intuitive user interface. On the left side, there are five menu items: Home, Create, Library, Explore, and Search (Figure 3.1).

To create a new song with SUNO, navigate to the Create menu item. There, on the left side, you'll find an input field titled "Song Description". In this field, you enter a simple description that outlines the desired style, atmosphere, or instrumentation of the song. After entering your description, a simple click on Create prompts SUNO to immediately generate two songs that match your description.

Figure 3.1 The Main Interface of SUNO's AI-Powered Music Creation Platform.

How to Formulate an Effective Text Prompt

The key to successfully using SUNO lies in the precise formulation of the so-called text prompt. Through my extensive experiments with SUNO, I've found that the system understands an astonishingly wide range of inputs—even entire sentences, and even in German. However, it's common practice to formulate prompts in English. The best approach is to use short, concise keywords separated by commas.

Here are some examples of prompts that have led to excellent results in the past:

- Energetic Latin dance, vibrant and rhythmic, catchy melody, summer vibes, featuring congas, trumpets, acoustic guitar
- Dark, fast to slow, industrial, bhangra, synthwave elements, spinning, moog out, clear vocals
- Guitar, trap, rap, deep layered bass, chill, dreamy

Emotional, sad, metalcore, progressive metalcore, modern

After SUNO creates two examples that vary in length between approximately two and four minutes, they appear with a small album cover and a title in the main area of the user interface. In the center of the album cover is a small triangle—a play button—that you can click to listen to the result. This way, you can easily decide which of the two versions you prefer.

Additional Features for Fine-Tuning the Result

SUNO offers numerous other features to influence the result precisely and tailor it even better to your wishes. One of these is located above the "Song Description" field: the Upload Audio button. Here, you can upload your own audio file to be used as the basis for the composition. This file could be an instrumental phrase, a few chords played on the piano or guitar, or even a vocal track. SUNO intelligently uses this uploaded material as a starting point and integrates it into its composition.

In my experiments, I was often pleasantly surprised at how well SUNO processes even the poorest-quality audio files to develop high-quality songs from them. Regardless of the quality of the uploaded file, the AI is remarkably capable of producing an impressive result based on a given idea—no matter how imperfect.

Next to the Upload Audio button is a dropdown menu that allows you to select the version of SUNO you want to work with. It's advisable to always use the latest version to benefit from the newest improvements and features. At the time of writing this book, the latest version was 3.5.

Other Settings

Above the "Song Description" field on the right, you'll find another button titled Instrumental. When this button is activated, SUNO generates a purely instrumental song without vocals. If it's not activated, the generated piece automatically includes vocals.

To the left of the Upload Audio button, there's another important button: Custom. When activated, additional fields for individual customization open up. One of these fields is the Lyrics field, where you can enter your own song lyrics. This way, you can provide the AI with predefined lyrics, which it then integrates into the song.

When entering your own song lyrics, it's advisable to clearly structure the song—into verse, bridge, and chorus. You achieve this by preceding each section of the text with a heading in square brackets, known as "square brackets." These markers not only help visually structure the song but also enable the AI to arrange the different parts of the song exactly as you wish. SUNO recognizes these structural cues and uses them to shape the song according to the specified sections.

Here are some examples of how to structure song lyrics with square brackets:

> [Intro] This is the intro that leads into the song…
> [Verse 1] This is the first verse of the song…
> [Chorus] This is the chorus that repeats…
> [Bridge] Here is the bridge that connects…
> [Verse 2] This is the second verse with more details…
> [Pre-Chorus] This is the pre-chorus that comes before the chorus…

By clearly labeling, SUNO can better understand and implement the different parts of the song, leading to a harmonious and well-structured composition.

Exploring Advanced Customizations

In my research for this book, I came across numerous ways to use the Lyrics field and square brackets to give SUNO specific instructions about song parts. Interestingly, SUNO doesn't offer a comprehensive user manual explaining all the possibilities, and not all inputs work 100% of the time. Nevertheless, it's worth experimenting with these options to gain more influence over the musical design of the song and provide the AI with targeted creative impulses.

Here are some examples of instructions that can be formulated in square brackets to influence the structure and style of the song:

[Sad Verse]—A verse with a sad mood.
[Happy Chorus]—A cheerful chorus.
[Short Instrumental Intro]—A short instrumental intro.
[Percussion Break]—A pause focusing on percussion.
[Melodic Bass]—A melodic bass part.
[Big Finish]—A grand, powerful finale.
[Fade Out]—A slow fade-out of the song at the end.

Additionally, you can influence the musical genre of a specific song part or the way the vocals sound. Using square brackets, you can give SUNO specific styles and sonic characteristics to further refine the creative process and achieve the desired musical expression.

Here are some examples of how to influence the genre or vocal style of a song part:

[Power Pop Chorus]—A chorus in the power pop style, sounding energetic and catchy.
[Bass Drop]—A section with a strong, deep bass drop, typically in EDM or dubstep style.

Beyond genres, there are instructions that can influence the mood or expression of the vocals:

[Shout]—A sung part that's more shouted or powerfully called out.
[Whimsical]—A part that sounds playful and imaginative.
[Melancholy]—A melancholic and thoughtful sound for the vocals or music.
[Rapped Verse]—A verse delivered in rap style.

Another important feature that SUNO offers is the use of parentheses () to distinguish certain vocal parts from the lead singer. Texts in parentheses are not interpreted by the lead singer but by a choir or an effected or filtered voice. This technique can be used to achieve creative effects, make the song more varied, or highlight specific text phrases.

Here's an example of how to use parentheses:

[Chorus]

We keep on running to the light
(We won't stop, we won't stop)

Through the darkness of the night
(Hold on tight, hold on tight)

Every step brings us closer
(Closer now, closer now)

Feel the fire burning brighter
(Feel the heat, feel the heat)

In this example, the chorus is sung solo, and at the end of each line, a choir responds with a short phrase in parentheses. This technique creates a call-and-response dynamic that makes the chorus more energetic and exciting, highlighting the collaboration between the lead singer and the choir.

Additional Features in Custom Mode

In Custom mode, we find the familiar Style of Music field below the Lyrics field, where we can describe the music style of the entire song with a text prompt, as previously discussed. This functionality remains unchanged in Custom mode and allows you to control the musical direction of the entire song.

An additional field available only in Custom mode is the Title field. Here, you can give the song a title in advance. This makes it easier to find the song later and gives it a distinct identity from the outset. An appropriate title can also serve as creative inspiration for the further process.

Functions After Song Generation: Sharing, Feedback, and Download

After SUNO has generated two songs based on our prompt, there are additional functions we can use to edit and share our creations besides listening to them.

An important function is EXTEND, which allows us to extend the song. We'll delve into this function shortly, as it offers many interesting options for expanding the composition.

Next is the PUBLIC function, a toggle switch we can activate to publish our song in the showcase of the SUNO website. When this switch is turned on, other users can listen to the song we've generated. This can be particularly useful for getting feedback from the community or simply sharing your works with others.

There's also the option to give feedback on the song in the form of a thumbs-up or thumbs-down. This allows us to inform SUNO how much we like the result and helps the AI improve its future suggestions.

The next button is COPY SONG LINK, which allows us to create a direct link to the generated song. This link can be sent to another person, who can then listen to the song. This is extremely convenient because we don't have to download and send the song as an MP3 file first. Instead, it's sufficient to pass on the song link so someone else can listen to the song directly through the platform.

The Three-Dot Menu: Advanced Song Editing Functions

To the right of the Copy Song Link button, you'll find the symbol with three dots ("…"). Behind these three dots are a variety of important functions that give you even more control over editing and downloading your songs.

Create Menu: Creative Tools for Song Expansion

In the Create menu, you'll find several options to further refine your song:

- Extend Function
  The Extend function in SUNO allows you to lengthen a clip or a complete song by adding more clips—up to one minute per clip. To extend a song or clip, click on the EXTEND button of the desired clip. This creates Part 2 from the original clip; from Part 2, you can extend to Part 3, from Part 3 to Part 4, and so on until the song reaches the desired end. Each extended section is marked next to the clip's name, and each extension generates two clips. If you regenerate a generation, even more variants may appear.

- Reuse Prompt
  This function in SUNO allows users to reuse the text prompt (the original description or instruction) used to create a particular song to generate their own songs. This function is especially useful if you're inspired by a song and want to use a similar mood or structure for your own composition.

- Cover Song
  This feature lets you transform your song or uploaded audio into a new genre or style while preserving the melody. It's a great way to reinterpret your songs.

- Get Stems

  The Get Stems function offers the possibility to download the individual stems (i.e., the separate tracks) of the song. This is particularly helpful if you want to further edit the song production or create your own mixes and remixes.

- Song Radio

  The Song Radio function in SUNO allows users to discover music that stylistically or thematically matches a selected song. When you use this function, SUNO creates a sort of "radio" experience around the song. This means that a playlist or sequence of songs is generated that share similar characteristics—like genre, style, mood, or other musical elements—based on the original track.

  This function helps users find new music that aligns with their current preferences or the mood of a particular song they've enjoyed. It's comparable to song-based radio stations on other music streaming platforms, where the algorithm selects songs that fit well together based on attributes like tempo, key, and mood.

Edit Menu: Adjust Song Details

In the Edit menu, you can further customize your song:

- Song Details

  With Song Details, you can change the title and album cover of the song to give it a personal touch or make it easier to recognize.

- Crop Song

  This function allows you to shorten the song. Select the part of the waveform you want to keep and cut away unnecessary sections.

- Add to Playlist

  This function lets you add your song to one of your playlists for easier access later.

Download Menu: Download Songs

The Download menu offers various options to download your song:

- MP3

  Download a compressed version of your song—perfect for easy sharing.

- WAV

  Choose the WAV format if you need maximum audio quality, for example, for further editing.

- Video

  If you want to download your song including the automatically generated video, this option is also available.

- Regenerate Video

  This function in SUNO AI allows users to update the automatically generated video for a song, especially if the title, song artwork, or displayed lyrics have changed. Instead of creating the video from scratch, you can quickly and easily generate a new version that reflects your changes.

Under the three dots, there's also the Share menu item, which offers additional options for sharing the generated song. Here, you'll find the Copy Link function again to forward the song as a direct link. This allows you to easily share the song with others without having to download it.

Additionally, there's the Share To function, which lets you share the song directly on platforms like X (formerly Twitter), Facebook, or via email. These options make it easy to spread the song across various channels and reach a broader audience, whether in social networks or through direct email dispatch.

Under the Download menu item, SUNO offers the option to download the generated song in various formats. The MP3 format is well-suited for sending the song to others, as the file size is significantly smaller than that of a WAV file. The WAV file, on the other hand, offers the best audio quality and is sensible if you want to further process the song in post-production, such as for mixing or mastering. There's also the option to download a video file of the song, which is useful if we want to post the song with visuals on social media.

Under Report, users can inform SUNO if they believe there was an error or bug in song generation or another function. This feature serves to provide feedback and contribute to the improvement of the platform.

The last function we find is Move To Trash, which allows you to delete a song from your library. This is useful if you want to remove songs that are no longer needed or that you don't want to save further.

When selecting an extended clip, the previous parts are highlighted and visible on the Create page. To seamlessly merge all extended parts into a single audio clip, click on the … button of the last clip and select the option Get Whole Song. This combines all parts into a complete song without additional credits being charged. The result is marked as Full Song.

Exploring Other Menu Items

The most important functions of SUNO are found under the Create menu item, as this is where you can create and customize your own music. Nevertheless,

I want to provide a brief overview of the other menu items that also offer useful features.

Under Home, you'll find a selection of songs from other users. This selection provides an excellent opportunity to get inspired and develop new ideas for your own music projects.

The Library menu item gives a good overview of your own music, including the songs you've published so that other users can listen to them. Here, you can organize your music into playlists and see if you've already gained followers with your music. It's a central place to manage and showcase your musical works.

With the Explore menu item, you can discover new music styles. A well-programmed random generator suggests various music styles that you can listen to in short excerpts. This function is particularly suitable for using new styles as a template for your next project and expanding your own creative horizon.

Under Search, you have the option to specifically search for songs from other users. This function makes it easier to find interesting music created by the community and can also serve as inspiration for your own works.

See Suno in Action

https://youtu.be/nyo6nUVfevk?si=6OHdywqb6TFP_uWf&t=40

UDIO: A New Platform for AI-Generated Music

The website udio.com was launched only a few months after suno.com and shows many conceptual similarities to the established Suno platform. The design of the website and the user experience are quite reminiscent of Suno, and the quality of the generated music tracks is similarly high. Whether Suno or UDIO is better is ultimately a matter of personal taste. In my tests, both platforms delivered excellent results, with each having its own strengths depending on the specific use case. However, many users who have tested both platforms have clearly favored UDIO. It's likely that each of these applications has its own unique advantages and weaknesses.

Nonetheless, I would like to provide you with an overview of how to use UDIO so you can form your own opinion.

Step One: Creating an Account

Like most programs or websites offering AI tools, the first step is to create a user account. After registration, the platform takes you directly to the main interface.

The User Interface of UDIO

On the left side of the interface, there are four main menus. The first item, Home, gives you an overview of examples that other users have created with UDIO. You can click on these examples to play them. If you want more information, you can click on the title in the playback bar at the bottom left. This opens a detailed view where you can see the prompt used to generate the piece of music. To the right of the prompt, there is an icon to copy it. So, if you particularly like a piece and want to create something similar, you can simply copy the prompt and use it as the basis for your own.

Creating Music with the "Create" Menu

The most exciting part, however, is under the "Create" menu—this is where the music literally comes to life. At the top of the page, you'll find an input field where you can type your prompt. Here, you can describe in detail what kind of song UDIO should create for you.

For beginners, it can be helpful to use the Randomize Prompt function—a dice icon to the left of the input field. This function gives you random suggestions for what such a text could look like. Alternatively, below the input field, there is a button labeled Suggestions, offering words and phrases that you can simply click on to add to your prompt.

A particularly useful feature of UDIO is its multilingual capability. Unlike many other AI music tools that only support English input, UDIO allows you to enter prompts in several languages, including German, French, Italian, and others. This means you can choose whichever language you feel most comfortable with for your creative input.

Tips for Creating Successful Prompts

A proven way to create prompts is by using keywords separated by commas. However, UDIO can also handle more complex, fully formulated sentences. Here are some examples of prompts that have already led to good results on UDIO:

- 2020s, youthful, indie pop, electropop, female vocalist
- Lofi, Chillhop, Japanese, Chill, lo-fi hip hop, instrumental hip hop, Guitar, Uptempo, chillstep, tranquil, guitar, sadness, dreaming, bittersweet, chilling, calm, melodic
- nu metal, alternative rock, melodic, rhythmic, female vocalist, electric guitar, ethereal, angelic vocals, passionate, atmospheric
- big band, jazz, swing, female vocalist, love song

After entering a prompt in UDIO and pressing the Create button, the platform immediately generates two suggestions on the right side of the interface.

These suggestions are based on the prompt you entered and represent two different interpretations by the AI. You can listen to these suggestions to decide if one of them meets your expectations or if you want to make further adjustments to the prompt to achieve a result that fits even better.

MUREKA: Creative Music Design via YouTube Link

New providers are continually entering the market, pursuing interesting and innovative approaches in the field of AI-assisted music production. One example is the webpage Mureka, which recently introduced an exciting feature. Users can now record a melody and use it as the foundation for a song. Moreover, Mureka allows the definition of the desired music style not only through text inputs but also by inserting a YouTube link to an existing song or even by uploading your own audio files. Particularly innovative is the approach that users can upload and sell the music they create with Mureka via an integrated online webshop. Unfortunately, the musical quality of the generated works still lags significantly behind platforms like SUNO and UDIO. However, this could change drastically with a single update, so it's worthwhile to keep an eye on this project.

In conclusion, I would like to mention that during my research, I have tested other tools, including the platforms MusicGen by Meta, SoundDRAW, and AIVA. These tools were presumably developed before SUNO and UDIO came to market and were the best available at the time. However, due to the advancements and possibilities that SUNO and UDIO offer today, these older tools have significantly lost relevance. For this reason, I have consciously decided not to cover them further in this book and to focus on the groundbreaking developments of SUNO and UDIO.

4 From Singer to Cyborg

The Evolution of the Human Voice through AI Technologies

Until now, music production, and especially vocal recording, was a complex process that posed both technical and creative challenges. In a typical recording studio, good room acoustics that allow as little reverb as possible ensure a clear recording. The recording engineer often sits in a separate room or wears headphones to minimize disturbances. High-quality microphones and the right positioning are essential to achieve the desired sound. Close proximity to the microphone makes the voice warmer and richer in bass, while a greater distance produces more room ambiance. In the past, it was important to compress the recording's dynamics to avoid clipping, but modern systems offer enough headroom and dynamic range to make this largely unnecessary. Nevertheless, care must be taken to ensure that even in the loudest passages, there remains a few dB of headroom.

After the first vocal track is recorded, there are various methods to create the best version. A common practice is comping, where multiple takes are recorded, and the best parts are assembled into a final track. In genres like ballads, a single, perfectly recorded track may be sufficient. For a fuller sound, doubling is often done, where the singer records the same passage multiple times. These doubles are then slightly lowered in volume and panned in the stereo field to create a wider sound. In addition to doubling, second and third harmonies or octaves can be added to make the vocals even richer and more complex. These additional voices can be recorded by the same singer or by different backup singers, depending on the desired sound.

A creative use of choirs can involve responding to the lead vocals or supporting them with harmonic pads on vowels like "Ooh," "Oh," or "Ah." After all vocal recordings are completed, the editing of the vocals begins. Here, intonation often takes center stage. Two proven tools are Auto-Tune and Melodyne. Auto-Tune automatically corrects the pitch to the nearest note of the set scale, delivering quick results. However, if more precise corrections are needed, Melodyne offers greater control by graphically displaying each note and allowing individual adjustments.

Besides intonation, timing is important. With time-stretching or warping functions, notes can be adjusted in position and length. Finally, audio effects

DOI: 10.4324/9781003621126-4

like compressors, equalizers, delay, and reverb are used to optimize the sound and integrate it into the overall track.

This was the traditional approach to vocal production. But today, artificial intelligence opens up entirely new possibilities. AI can not only revolutionize vocal recording and editing but also support creative processes and unlock new sound worlds.

Artificial intelligence today offers numerous ways to optimize this process or design it entirely differently. These possibilities can be roughly divided into two categories. First, we can change the voice of an existing vocal so that it sounds as if another singer had performed it. This means any of us can record our own voice and then transform it to sound like Whitney Houston, Michael Jackson, Lady Gaga, or Ed Sheeran. The platform lalals.com specializes in this function. The problem with the voices of these stars is often that the training material used isn't always sufficient, so the result isn't 100% optimal. However, many singers have now been brought into the studio to sing specifically for AI voice samples, making these recordings technically very good.

The second possibility is to generate vocals from scratch on the computer. For this, a piano roll is used, where each note can be created with the mouse. Then you insert the text into these notes and can adjust parameters like vibrato, volume, and expression until the result is pleasing. In the past, the results of this technique were often very unnatural and sounded electronic. But the quality of these voices has improved enormously.

An example of this is a documentary by the TV channel 3SAT about AI in music, in which I was featured as a music producer. In an experiment, I played some of my productions to the well-known Austrian singer Monika Ballwein, and she had to guess whether the vocals were produced by real humans or generated by AI. To my great surprise, she was wrong about 80% of the time. This shows that the quality of AI voices is now so good that even professionals often can't tell the difference.

An exciting possibility is also to digitize your own singing—to create a model of your own voice. Afterwards, you can transform a cappella recordings of Madonna or Ed Sheeran into your own voice and hear how you would have sung those songs.

In this chapter, I provide an overview of the most important tools available today to generate or edit vocals using artificial intelligence. I explain in detail how to work with plugins like Synthesizer V or software like Audiamus to generate vocals from scratch, or how to use ACE Studio or lalal.ai to modify existing vocals so that they sound like another person. I also give a brief introduction to the established tool ElevenLabs for speech synthesis.

I hope you have a lot of fun discovering these fascinating new possibilities in music production!

Synthesizer V—AI-Generated Vocals

Synthesizer V by Dreamtonics is a plugin used in music programs like Ableton Live or Logic Pro to generate vocals. By opening the plugin, you access a piano roll—a note editor that displays pitches from bottom to top and time from left to right. You can create notes with a double-click, which can be lengthened or shortened by dragging the right edge. Playback starts by clicking the play button or pressing the spacebar. Initially, the entered notes are played only by a synthesizer. However, under the track name, you can select a singer who will initially sing all notes with the text "lalala." By double-clicking on a note, you can enter the text or word for that specific note.

There are two important tricks you should know:

1 Words with Multiple Syllables: Write the entire word into the first note, and insert a "+" in the subsequent notes to indicate that the next syllable should be sung on the note with the plus sign. For example, for the word "Elephant," which requires three notes, write the entire word "Elephant" into the first note and place a "+" in the second and third notes.
2 Extending a Syllable Over Multiple Notes: Sometimes you want to sing a single syllable over several notes. To do this, write the word into the first note and insert a "-" into each following note. For example, if you want to sing the word "love" over three notes, write "Love" into the first note and a "-" into the two subsequent notes.

Below the piano roll, you can open the Parameters field to input parameters like pitch, vibrato, volume, and other functions in the form of curves. On the right side of the plugin, you can open various windows to make different settings for selected notes or the entire track. For example, you can convert selected notes into so-called "rap notes" to make Synthesizer V perform rap vocals.

You can also implement choirs quickly and easily: simply duplicate the first track, select all the notes on the new track, right-click on a note, and choose the "Generate a New Take" function. This creates the impression of two singers singing together. You can repeat this trick as often as you like, and of course, you can shift the notes of the new track to a different pitch to create second and third harmonies.

Currently, there are voices available for English, Japanese, Chinese, and Cantonese languages, both male and female. Unfortunately, a German-singing voice is not yet available. My preferred voices include Solaria for female vocals and Saros for male vocals.

Synthesizer V costs €86.02

See Synthesizer V in Action

https://youtu.be/nyo6nUVfevk?si=91DvmONtch9hU-FO&t=88

ACE Studio

ACE Studio is software for Mac or Windows that allows you to generate vocals. There are various options available:

- Create Notes Manually: You can create notes using your mouse.
- Import MIDI Files: Bring in a MIDI file and insert lyrics into these notes.
- Import Acapella Recordings: Import your own acapella recordings, which are automatically converted into notes with lyrics.

After importing or creating your notes, you can modify the lyrics, melody, or even the voice. Multiple voices are available in English, Japanese, and Chinese, and it's possible to create new voices by combining existing ones. For an additional fee, you can even create a custom voice model of your own voice, allowing the generated vocals to be sung in your voice, either via mouse input or audio import.

Creating Vocals with the Mouse in ACE Studio

Follow these steps to create new vocals:

1 Create a Singer Track: Upon opening ACE Studio, a Singer Track should already be present. If not, click the plus symbol (+) under the tracks to add one.
2 Create a Clip: Double-click in the timeline area of the Singer Track to create an empty clip.
3 Open the Piano Roll: After creating the clip, a piano roll will appear at the bottom of the screen. Time progresses from left to right, and pitch is displayed from bottom to top.
4 Draw Notes:
Draw Select Tool: Using the default "Draw Select" tool, double-click in the piano roll to create notes. Adjust the note length by clicking and dragging the right edge of the note.
Draw Note Tool: For a quicker method, select the "Draw Note" (pencil) tool. Click and drag to the right to set the note's length as you create it.
5 Enter Lyrics:
Single Note: Double-click on a note to input a syllable.
Multiple Notes: Select multiple notes, press Cmd + E (Edit Lyrics), and type your lyrics into the input field.

Singing a Syllable Over Multiple Notes

There are two methods to extend a syllable over several notes:

1 Note Split (Scissors Tool):

- Select the "Note Split" (scissors) tool.
- Split a longer note into multiple shorter notes.
- Adjust the pitches of the new notes as needed.

2 Using Hyphens:

- Add additional notes where needed.
- Insert a hyphen (-) in the text of the subsequent notes.
- This indicates that these notes continue the previous syllable.

Advanced Controls

Additional mouse functions and a window in the lower section allow you to adjust parameters like vibrato, energy, formant, falsetto, and more, giving you detailed control over the vocal performance.

Working with Audio Tracks

ACE Studio also includes Audio Tracks where you can record or import audio. This feature lets you:

- Add a playback track: incorporate instrumental tracks to accompany your vocals.
- Use a reference song: import a song to guide your composition.
- Convert your own acapella recordings:
- Import your own acapella recording.
- Right-click the audio file, navigate to the AI Plugin menu, and select "Acapella Convert."
- Your vocal recording is converted into editable notes.
- Modify the notes, pitch, and even change the voice to experiment creatively.

Note: Always ensure you have the necessary rights and permissions when using any audio material.

Creating Vocal Doubles and Choirs

Doubling vocals is a common technique to enrich the sound:

- Vocal Doubles:
- Right-click on a clip in a Singer Track.

- Select "Create Vocal Doubles for This Track."
- This creates duplicates that can be panned left and right for a fuller effect.
- Building Choirs:
- Apply the doubling function multiple times.
- Change the voices on the new tracks.
- Layer them to construct complete choral arrangements.

Pricing: ACE Studio costs $22 per month.

By leveraging ACE Studio's powerful features, you can craft intricate vocal performances, experiment with different voices, and enhance your music productions—all within a single platform.

Audimee—Transforming Vocal Sounds

At Audimee.com, you can upload an acapella track and convert it into a different voice (Figure 4.1). A wide selection of studio singers is available for this purpose, and the results are of outstanding quality. In addition to the singers offered by Audimee, you can also create a voice model of your own voice. To do this, you upload at least 20 minutes of your own singing, ideally in studio quality and without effects like reverb and delay. After about 90 minutes, your personalized voice model will be ready. This means you could, for example, hear how a song would sound with your own voice, even if you've never sung it yourself. I tested this myself, and although the result is impressive, the quality doesn't seem as high as with the voices provided by Audimee. In my YouTube video, you can judge for yourself.

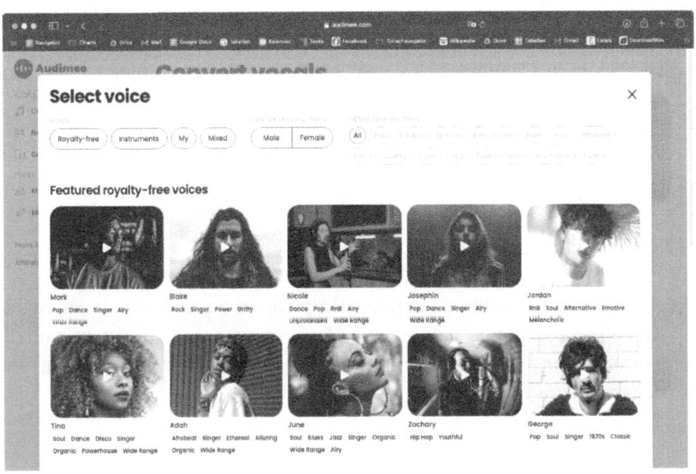

Figure 4.1 Audimee's Interface for Selecting Royalty-Free Vocal Models.

Steps to Convert Your Voice

1 Create an Account and Choose a Plan:
Options include Free, Starter, Pro, or Ultimate.
2 Navigate to "Convert Vocals."
3 Select the Desired Voice.
4 Upload Your Audio Under "Input":
The audio should not contain music or audio effects like reverb or delay.
    - If your acapella does have effects or background music, Audimee offers AI-powered functions to remove them (e.g., "Remove instrumental," "Remove background vocals," "Remove reverb and echo," "Remove noise"). However, based on my experience, the quality of the result may suffer.
5 Click on "Convert":
This process takes about one to two minutes.
6 Retrieve Your Result Under "Output":
The converted audio can be downloaded from here.

Additional Features

Audimee offers other AI-assisted functions. For example, you can upload a song and extract only the vocals or only the instrumental track. You can create new vocal models by mixing existing voices or by uploading your own audio material to generate a new vocal model.

Subscription Plans

- Free: $0
- Upload up to 15 minutes of vocals for free and test Audimee's features.
- Starter: $12 per month
- Upload up to one hour of vocals per month.
- Pro: $25 per month
- Upload up to ten hours of vocals per month.
- Ultimate: $49 per month
- Upload unlimited vocals per month.

If you commit to a yearly subscription, the prices become even more favorable.

By utilizing Audimee's innovative platform, you can experiment with different vocal transformations and explore new creative possibilities in your music production workflow.

See Audimee in Action

https://youtu.be/nyo6nUVfevk?si=rXxGsxJ4GclXUxXx&t=143

Lalals.com—Sing Like the Stars

The basic idea of Lalals is very simple: upload your voice and convert it so that it sounds like Ed Sheeran, The Weeknd, Dua Lipa, or another famous singer. Lalals guarantees that you can publish songs using these voices without violating copyright laws. In addition to the many stars, there are also studio singers—vocalists you might not know—who are identified only by their first names, such as Leyla, Luke, Miles, Noemi, and Alba (Figure 4.2).

These voices are of even higher quality because they have more audio material available that was used to train the AI. So if you're not aiming to imitate a well-known star, I always recommend using these voices. Here are some tips from my experience:

1 Use the Highest Quality Recordings Possible

   The better the original, the better the AI can work, and the better the result will be.

2 Ensure Your Uploaded Audio Has No Effects

   The audio file you upload should not have effects like reverb or delay, no additional voices like doubles or backing vocals, and no background music. While there are functions to remove these, the end result may suffer in quality.

3 Match the Original Performance to the Desired Singer

   If you want the result to sound like a famous singer, try to make your original recording sound as similar as possible to that singer. Lalals changes the timbre of the voice, but to truly mimic a well-known star, the interpretation should be as similar as possible.

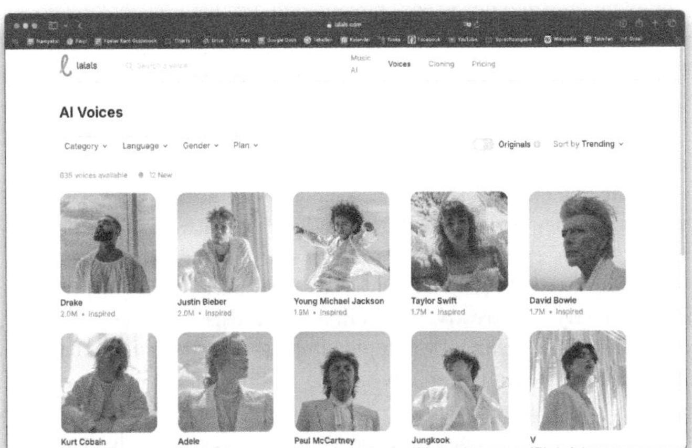

Figure 4.2 Lalals' Platform Showcasing AI-Generated Celebrity-Inspired Voices.

4 Avoid Mistakes in Pronunciation, Timing, or Intonation

If the audio file you upload has errors in pronunciation, timing, or intonation, these will also appear in the result. Make sure your original recording is performed as professionally as possible.

Subscription Options for Lalals

- Free: No Cost

  The free version is heavily limited and offers only minimal enjoyment. Audio files can be up to 3 minutes long, and the conversion process takes quite a while.
- Basic: $12 per Month

  Up to 100 conversions per month
  Access to a limited selection of voices
- Pro: $24 per Month

  Up to 500 conversions per month
  Access to all available voices
- Studio: $99 per Month

  No limitations

By following these tips and choosing the right subscription plan, you can make the most out of Lalals and explore new creative possibilities in your music production workflow.

Vocoflex—Sing Like Whitney Houston Live on Stage

Vocoflex by Dreamtonics is an innovative plugin that transfers the characteristics of one voice to another. At first glance, this might sound similar to functions offered by other programs we've mentioned in this chapter. However, Vocoflex stands out due to some crucial features: the transformation happens in real-time with an extremely low latency of only 35 milliseconds. This speed allows it to be used in live performances without any noticeable delay.

Imagine standing on stage and seamlessly switching between the vocal timbres of Britney Spears, Adele, and Whitney Houston while singing. With Vocoflex, this is exactly possible—and it's continuous. This means you can fluidly transition between different vocal characters during a performance, offering entirely new creative possibilities for artists.

In my extensive testing, I was highly impressed by the plugin's capabilities. However, there are limitations. While the timbre of the voice is successfully transferred, many other characteristic features of a singer remain unchanged. For example, the raspy quality of Joe Cocker's voice or the distinctive grit in Michael Jackson's high, aggressive range are lost. Individual pronunciation, the way notes are articulated, and the use of vibrato—all elements contributing to a voice's uniqueness—remain unaffected.

These limitations do not diminish the potential of Vocoflex. It's excellent for situations where one person wants to simulate an entire choir that sounds like 20 different people singing. Here's how you can achieve that.

Important Considerations When Using Vocoflex

- As with most AI-based tools, a crucial rule applies to Vocoflex: the better the source material, the better the result. This means:
- High-Quality Recording: The voice should be recorded at the highest possible quality.
- Talent Matters: The more skilled the singer, the more impressive the outcome.
- Clean Audio: Ensure no effects like reverb or delay are applied, and the recording is free from background noises such as other voices or instruments.

Getting Started with Voice Transformation

To use Vocoflex:

1 Insert the Plugin: Place Vocoflex on the track containing the vocals you wish to alter.
2 Import a Vocal Sample: Drag a vocal file (minimum of ten seconds long) into the plugin. Vocoflex will analyze the material in a few seconds.
3 Explore the Voice Map: A line with multiple points will appear, representing different sound components of the voice. Move your mouse along this line to audition various vocal transformations.

Pitch Variation

In the lower-left corner of the software, there's a control to adjust the pitch of the voice:

- Changing Gender Characteristics: Raising the pitch by 7–12 semitones can transform a male voice into a female-sounding voice, producing realistic results.
- Key Considerations: Adjustments other than ±12 semitones (an octave) will change the key of the vocals, which may cause them to clash with the rest of your song or arrangement.

Using Pre-made Voices

Vocoflex offers a variety of pre-made voices:

- Mai Presets: Access these in the "Mai Presets" menu. They appear as lines with points in the interface.

- Blending Voices: Move your mouse not only along one line but also between two lines to create a blended sound.
- Subtractive Mixing: It's possible to move along the backside of a line to subtract elements of the other voice.

This functionality is intuitive—experiment with different positions on the screen and let your ears guide you to the best sound.

Voice Changer Navigator

- Another feature is the "Voice Changer Navigator," which allows you to:
- Adjust Gender Characteristics: Vary the sound on an X-axis between male and female.
- Influence Timbre: Modify the tonal quality on a Y-axis.
- Generate New Voices: Use the randomizer to create entirely new vocal characteristics.

Simulating a Choir with Vocoflex

To simulate a choir with Vocoflex:

1 Understand Variations in a Choir: In a real choir, differences between v voices include:
    - Pitch variations
    - Pitch fluctuations within notes
    - Volume differences
    - Timing discrepancies
    - Note lengths
    - Pronunciation nuances
    - Unique timbres
2 Record Multiple Takes: Have your singer perform the melody multiple times—once for each desired choir voice (e.g., 10 times for 10 voices).
3 Apply Vocoflex Individually:
    - Place Vocoflex on each vocal track.
    - Select a different voice preset for each track to simulate diverse choir members.
4 Create Multi-Part Harmonies: Repeat this process for additional harmony parts to build a rich, multi-layered choir.

Practical Tips

- Experiment Freely: Don't hesitate to try different settings and presets to discover unique sounds.

- Listen Critically: Use your ears to judge the best combinations and adjustments.
- Maintain Musical Cohesion: Be mindful of key and timing to ensure the transformed vocals fit seamlessly into your project.

Pricing: Vocoflex costs $159 (approximately €145).

By leveraging Vocoflex's advanced capabilities, you can unlock new creative avenues in your music production, from live vocal transformations to crafting expansive virtual choirs—all with remarkable ease and realism.

Sound ID Voice AI—The AI in a Plugin

Throughout this book, we've introduced various tools, programs, and web applications that utilize artificial intelligence to generate or modify vocals. Late in the final phase of my work, I received a test license for the plugin SoundID Voice AI by Sonarworks. Although I haven't had extensive practical experience with it yet, my initial tests with this plugin have left a strong impression.

Why This Plugin?

A significant advantage of SoundID Voice AI is its seamless integration into the production workflow. There's no need to export audio files, upload them to a web platform, download them again, and then re-import them into your DAW (Digital Audio Workstation). Instead, the plugin allows for direct conversion of vocals within the DAW itself, greatly simplifying the workflow.

The sound quality of the generated voices is excellent, and the options are diverse: from soulful to rock, male to female—even voices of children and adolescents are available. I find this wide range to be a real enrichment to the creative process.

Experimental Possibilities and Limitations

Beyond voice conversion, SoundID Voice AI offers the ability to transform any voice or other audio signals into instrumental sounds like violin, saxophone, trumpet, and more. These functions can be found under the "Creative" category. While I consider this option experimental and entertaining, the quality of the resulting instrument sounds isn't on the level of a real musician. Therefore, I view this feature more as a novelty. Nonetheless, this doesn't detract from the plugin's main strength: high-quality vocal conversion.

Step-by-Step Guide to Voice Conversion

To convert vocals using SoundID Voice AI, follow these steps:

1. Add the Plugin: Insert SoundID Voice AI onto the track containing the vocals you wish to convert.
2. Capture the Vocals: Open the plugin and activate the "Capture" function. Start playback to record the vocals into the plugin.
3. Select a Voice: Choose your desired target voice from the list. Each time you click on a voice, a short audio sample plays to give you an idea of the end result.
4. Start the Conversion: Click "Start Processing" to initiate the transformation.

In my tests, converting material between 10 and 20 seconds long took about 30 seconds. So, the conversion time is generally longer than the actual audio length.

Additional Features and Settings

SoundID Voice AI offers other useful functions:

- AI Voice Enabled: This allows you to quickly compare the original vocal with the processed result.
- Transpose Function: Set to "Auto" by default, it automatically adjusts the pitch—for example, converting a female voice into a male voice an octave lower. You can disable this feature to manually adjust the pitch in semi-tones, giving you precise control over the final sound.

Conclusion

Although my experience with SoundID Voice AI is currently based on brief tests, the results have been convincing. It could very well become my preferred tool for vocal conversion, thanks to its quality and ease of use.

Pricing

For €39.99, you receive 180,000 tokens, which corresponds to approximately 300 minutes of audio material for conversion.

By integrating SoundID Voice AI into your workflow, you can explore new creative avenues in vocal production without leaving your DAW, making the process both efficient and inspiring.

ElevenLabs: The Future of Computer-Generated Speech

ElevenLabs is currently one of the leading tools for generating and editing computer-generated voices. The software not only offers outstanding quality in converting text to speech but also allows for impressive modification and customization of voices. Its intuitive menus and diverse settings make ElevenLabs the preferred tool for professionals in music and audio production (Figure 4.3).

Text to Speech

After logging in, ElevenLabs provides a variety of functions, with the "Text to Speech" menu being perhaps the most important. Here, you can enter text, select a voice, and click on "Generate Speech." Within seconds, the text is converted into realistic-sounding speech that can be downloaded directly. The software supports not only English and German but also 28 other languages, all of which are of high quality.

Voice Changer

Another highlight is the "Voice Changer," which allows you to upload an audio file and convert it into a different voice while retaining the speed, pitch,

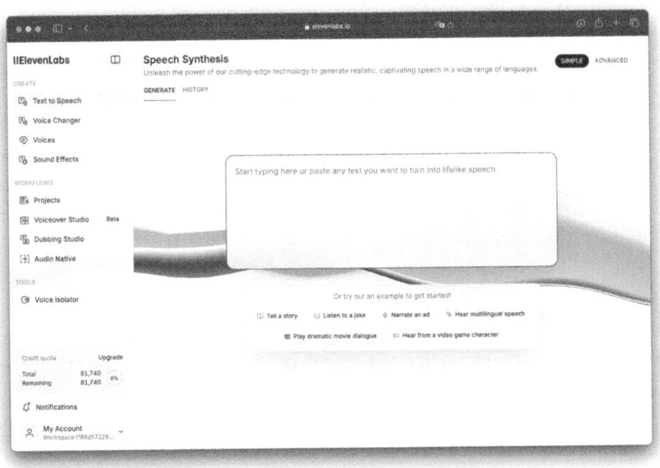

Figure 4.3 The Intuitive Interface of ElevenLabs for Text-to-Speech and Voice Customization.

and emotion of the original recording. Users can also generate their own voices by uploading voice samples.

Settings and Hacks

Furthermore, there are advanced settings that let you fine-tune the generated speech. Sliders for "Stability," "Similarity," and "Style Exaggeration" enable you to adjust the emotion and style of the voices. There are also so-called "hacks," such as inserting commands to control pauses or adjust pronunciation. These small tricks provide precise control over the nuances of the generated speech, making the results sound even more natural.

Fine-Tuning for Customized Speech Generation

ElevenLabs offers the ability to further refine how a voice speaks through advanced settings. By clicking on "Advanced" or adjusting the "Settings," you can modify parameters like Stability, Similarity, and Style Exaggeration to achieve the desired effect.

- Stability Slider: Influences how stable and consistent the voice sounds. A lower setting leads to a wider range of emotions and expressions, while a higher setting makes the voice more stable and monotonous. For livelier and more dramatic speech renditions, you can set the stability lower and try different generations until you reach the desired result.
- Similarity Slider: In Text-to-Speech (TTS) mode, it ensures that the generated voice remains consistent in its characteristics when generating the same text multiple times. In Voice Changer mode, it controls how precisely the AI mimics the nuances of an uploaded original voice. At a high setting, unwanted noises or artifacts from the original recording may be transferred.
- Style Exaggeration: Enhances the speaker's style. Although this function is usually left at 0, you can experiment with it to achieve stronger emphasis and stylistic variation.

Inserting Pauses

To integrate pauses into generated speech output, you can use the "break time" command. This allows you to determine the duration of the pause, improving the naturalness of the speech. For example, you could insert a 1.5-second pause by specifying:

<break time="1.5s"/>

This lets you adjust the pause duration and control the flow and emphasis of the speech.

Adjusting Pronunciation

To influence the pronunciation of individual words, use the **phoneme** command. This employs the International Phonetic Alphabet (IPA) to specify the exact phonetic transcription of the word. An example could be:

<phoneme alphabet="ipa" ph="your-IPA-Pronunciation-here">word</phoneme>

This ensures that specific words are pronounced exactly as you wish, which is particularly helpful for foreign words or names.

Controlling Emotions

A useful trick to influence the emotions of a sentence is to add the desired emotion in the form of narrative text. For example, you might write:

> "I hate spaghetti!" he shouted angrily.

Although the addition "he shouted angrily" needs to be removed from the generated speech output afterward, it affects how the sentence "I hate spaghetti!" is spoken—namely, aggressively and emotionally charged. This approach allows targeted control of tone and expression, making the generated speech even more authentic and human-like.

Voices: Creating and Customizing New Voices

Under the "Voices" menu, ElevenLabs provides an overview of all available voices. Users can use the "Add New Voice" function to generate their own voices. Four different options are available:

1 Voice Design: Utilize various menus and settings to create a new, individual voice. This option allows you to specifically adjust and personalize the characteristics of a voice.
2 Voice Library: This extensive library contains all the voices created by other subscribers in the community. Users can browse through the library and look for interesting voices suitable for their projects.
3 Voice Cloning: This feature enables you to clone a voice from an audio recording of a speaker using artificial intelligence. You upload a voice recording, from which a new synthetic voice is generated.

   A remarkable example of using such technology is the new production of the Bavarian series Pumuckl. Since the original voice actor, Hans Clarin, has passed away, his distinctive voice was reconstructed using artificial intelligence. The new actor first recorded Pumuckl's voice, which was then processed with AI to sound like Hans Clarin's original voice.

Although it's not known which specific tool was used, this approach involves similar voice cloning technology as offered by ElevenLabs and other providers. However, this method raises ethical questions, particularly concerning deepfakes and the possibility of attributing statements to people that they never made.

4 Instant and Professional Voice Cloning**: There are two versions of Voice Cloning:

Instant Voice Cloning works with a one-minute recording and delivers relatively good results quickly.

Professional Voice Cloning** requires a larger amount of voice material and has a processing time of about two weeks but provides the highest quality results. This method is particularly suitable for professional projects where utmost authenticity is required.

These features offer extensive possibilities to enrich your creative projects with unique voices or to clone and customize existing voices.

Sound Effects

In the "Sound Effects" menu, you can generate a variety of sounds using text prompts. A simple example could be:

> "A Porsche drives into a house wall."

This command generates a sound effect depicting a scene where a Porsche crashes into a house wall. The results are often surprisingly creative and can serve as a foundation for audio productions.

Alex Lauder, a producer friend from BAYERN 3, an Austrian radiostation, shared some interesting examples of how he used the Sound Effects function to create special voices:

Crowd shouting the German words "Thomas Foster": A prompt used to generate a crowd chant. Although not all generated results were perfect, he was able to find a recording that convincingly sounded like a crowd loudly shouting "Thomas Foster."

A demon saying the words 'I am here to kill you': This prompt aims for a creepy and threatening voice speaking sinister words. The result was impressive and created an eerie atmosphere.

With these advanced functions and commands, ElevenLabs provides deep control over the audio output, allowing users to achieve highly specialized and customized results that meet the individual requirements of their projects.

Projects: Flexible Work with Multiple Voices

Under the "Projects" menu, ElevenLabs offers the ability to create a new project where longer texts can be assigned to different voices. You can upload a text and then specifically select individual lines or paragraphs to be spoken by different voices. This function is particularly useful when working on more complex projects that require multiple speakers or characters.

VoiceLab Studio: Working Like in a DAW

An innovative extension of this concept is the new **VoiceLab Studio**. This function also allows you to work with multiple voices, and the workflow resembles a Digital Audio Workstation (DAW), where multiple audio tracks can be created and edited in parallel. In VoiceLab Studio, you can create different tracks for different voices and edit them precisely, allowing flexible control over voice recordings and seamless integration of different speakers.

Dubbing Studio: Seamless Translations with Your Own Voice

Additionally, there is the "Dubbing Studio" feature, which can be used for dubbing and translations. Here, you can upload your own voice in German and then generate a translation into another language, such as English. The special aspect is that the generated voice retains the same timbre and style of the original voice, enabling a seamless and natural-sounding translation. This translated speech output can then be downloaded and used in various projects.

Audio Native: Speech Playback for Your Webpage

Under the **"Audio Native"** menu, ElevenLabs offers the ability to embed an audio player on a website that reads the page's text using ElevenLabs' Text-to-Speech service. This allows visitors to listen to the content of a webpage instead of reading it. The integration is extremely simple and can be implemented with a short HTML code snippet.

Voice Isolator: Minimizing Background Noise

The "Voice Isolator" menu allows you to edit voice recordings that have disturbing background noises. This function isolates the voice from the background sounds, making it clear and free of disturbances. A typical example would be the post-processing of a film scene shot next to a busy highway. In this case, the Voice Isolator could be used to filter out the sounds of the highway and obtain a clean voice recording.

With its versatile and innovative functions, ElevenLabs offers a comprehensive platform for voice and audio production, catering to both creative professionals and businesses. Whether for automatic narration of websites, editing voice recordings, or creating complex voiceover projects—ElevenLabs opens up new possibilities in audiovisual design and elevates the use of artificial intelligence in this field to a new level.

Pricing: ElevenLabs starts at **$5 per month**.

See Eleven Labs in Action

https://youtu.be/nyo6nUVfevk?si=igDUU-HCs9RnPQuu&t=205

5 Audio Processing and Optimization

AI Technologies for Clear Sound

Technical errors in audio recordings cannot always be avoided. Especially in outdoor recordings, there are many challenges: excessive reverberation or too much background noise. But even in studio recordings, problems can occur that impair sound quality: overly strong breathing noises, the sliding of the hand on the guitar fretboard, clicks and rattling noises, and much more. In the past, these errors were very difficult or time-consuming to correct. The available tools were essentially limited to volume adjustments and equalizers.

Here, artificial intelligence opens up a completely new chapter and offers solutions for almost all of these problems. But how do you teach an AI to remove reverberation from a recording, for example?

You train a neural network by showing it many speech recordings with and without reverberation. The model learns to remove the reverb by comparing its results with the original recordings without reverb and adjusting its parameters to improve continuously. When the model is well-trained, it can be applied to new, reverberant speech recordings and outputs a version that is as free of reverberation as possible.

In this chapter, we will take a detailed look at various AI-powered tools specifically developed for error correction in audio recordings. We will examine their functionality, areas of application, and the benefits they offer to users. The tools discussed include Adobe Podcast, RX11 by iZotope, the Pure Bundle, and various applications for separating vocals and music, such as Lalal.ai.

Adobe Podcast

Adobe Podcast is a powerful tool that analyzes and optimizes speech recordings using AI. It can automatically remove background noise, enhance the sound of the voice, and minimize distracting noises. This is particularly useful for podcasters and content creators who record in less controlled environments but still want to achieve professional audio quality.

DOI: 10.4324/9781003621126-5

RX11 by iZotope

RX11 by iZotope is an advanced tool for audio restoration. It utilizes machine learning to detect and correct various types of audio errors. This includes removing clicks, pops, noise, and other unwanted sounds. RX11 offers specialized modules for different tasks and is an indispensable tool for sound engineers and audio professionals.

Pure Bundle

The Pure Bundle encompasses a series of tools specialized in improving audio quality. Using AI algorithms, these tools analyze audio data and make automatic adjustments to ensure clarity and purity of sound. They are particularly helpful in noise removal, sound enhancement, and dynamic processing.

Dyn Assist Pro

DynAssist Pro is a remarkable tool for audio processing that employs artificial intelligence to automatically distinguish between spoken words, breathing noises, pauses, and sibilant sounds in speech recordings. It then uses intelligent volume automation to optimize the dynamics of the recording:

- Adjusting Speech Volume: Loud passages are gently lowered, while quiet passages are raised to create a consistent and pleasant listening experience.
- Reducing Unwanted Noises: Disturbing sounds like breaths and overemphasized sibilants are selectively reduced in volume without altering the natural timbre of the voice.

By automating these adjustments, DynAssist Pro significantly improves the intelligibility and professionalism of speech recordings. The tool not only saves time in post-production but also enables less experienced users to achieve high-quality results. It is particularly useful for podcasters, voice-over artists, and anyone who regularly works with speech recordings and values clear and balanced sound.

Separation of Vocals and Music

Separating vocals and music is a challenging task that has been significantly simplified by AI-based tools. Software like Logic Pro offers advanced functions for isolating vocal tracks and musical accompaniment. These tools use deep learning algorithms to identify and separate different audio signals, facilitating remixing, sampling, and other creative processes.

The integration of artificial intelligence into audio production has revolutionized the possibilities for error correction and sound optimization. With tools like Adobe Podcast, RX11 by iZotope, the Pure Bundle, and applications for separating vocals and music, audio producers and technicians have powerful tools at their disposal that significantly improve both the quality and efficiency of their work. These technologies pave the way for new creative possibilities and set new standards in audio quality.

Adobe Podcast Saves Almost Any Voice Recording

For podcasts, high-quality voice recordings are of crucial importance. Clear and understandable sound quality not only enhances comprehension but is also essential for the professional image of the podcast. A recording that is reverberant, noisy, or filled with static appears unprofessional and diminishes the content's quality. In practice, however, it can be challenging to ensure optimal recording conditions, especially when conducting interviews with people who may not have the right technical equipment. Often, you're just grateful that the person has taken the time at all and have to make do with the given circumstances—be it a reverberant living room or disruptive background noises from open windows or other sources.

A few years ago, conventional audio editing tools like noise gates or equalizers would have allowed only limited improvements. But thanks to artificial intelligence, much is possible today that previously seemed unthinkable. With just a few clicks on podcast.adobe.com, you can upload your audio files and benefit from impressive AI-assisted audio processing. The AI technology significantly reduces disruptive background noises like voices, cars, or static and minimizes reverberation almost entirely. The result is impressive and greatly enhances the quality of your recordings.

With a free account, you can upload files up to 30 minutes in length (maximum 500 MB) per day. Premium accounts offer higher limits and also allow the uploading of video files.

Adobe Podcast costs $11.99 per month

By leveraging Adobe Podcast's advanced features, podcasters and content creators can achieve professional audio quality even in less-than-ideal recording environments.

See Adobe Podcast in Action

https://youtu.be/nyo6nUVfevk?si=taiA6jQK8J-q0GAF&t=230

RX 11 by iZotope

RX 11 utilizes advanced artificial intelligence to edit audio in a multitude of ways. Simply drag your audio file into the RX 11 window, and then you can choose from a variety of functions listed on the right side of the window to repair or edit the audio. With the "Preview" function, you can listen to the end result. To apply the editing, use the "Render" function. Once the processing is complete, you can export the final audio using the "Export" option in the File menu. Here is an overview of the most important features:

Breath Control

Anyone who regularly records speech knows the problem: breathing noises are usually too loud, and the more you focus on them, the more distracting they become. The Breath Control module offers a simple solution to this issue.

In the Breath Control module, you'll find a slider called "Target Level," which allows you to set the desired volume of the breathing noises. This slider enables you to reduce the breathing sounds to a natural and unobtrusive level without removing them entirely. This saves an incredible amount of time when editing audiobooks, podcasts, and other speech recordings.

De-bleed

When recording a concert with multiple microphones, significant bleed often occurs. For example, in the recording of a singer-songwriter, you often find some guitar in the vocal microphone and vice versa. The De-bleed module in RX 11 can quickly fix this problem.

Steps to Use the De-bleed Module

1 Select Source Track: Choose the track that contains the bleed you want to remove.
2 Select Bleed Track: Choose the track from which the bleed originates.
3 Learn: The De-bleed module analyzes the relationship between the two tracks to identify the bleed.
4 Adjust: Set the parameters to optimize the reduction of the bleed.
5 Render: Apply the settings to reduce the bleed in the source track.

This process results in clearer and better-separated recordings of vocals and instruments.

De-ess

In many speech and vocal recordings, the "s" and sibilant sounds are unpleasantly loud. The De-ess module provides a remedy.

Using the De-ess Module

- Adjust Threshold: Lower the Threshold slider to reduce the volume of "s" and sibilant sounds. The threshold determines the level at which the reduction of these sounds begins.

De-reverb

In voice recordings made in rooms not specifically designed for recording, there is often too much reverb on the voice. This is particularly problematic in film recordings where the microphone must maintain distance from the actors due to framing. The De-reverb module offers a solution. Increasing the Reduction slider decreases the amount of reverb heard. The slider controls the intensity of the reverb reduction.

Music Rebalance

Do you want to extract the a cappella version or the playback from a song? Then the Music Rebalance module is just right for you. With this module, you can individually adjust the volume of vocals, bass, drums, and the remaining instruments.

Imagine you want to create a playback of a song. All you need to do is pull the Vocal slider all the way down. This removes the vocal tracks while leaving the other elements of the song unchanged. You can leave the sliders for bass, drums, and other instruments at their default positions or adjust them as desired.

Overview of All Modules

- Ambience Match
- Azimuth
- Breath Control
- Center Extract
- De-bleed
- De-click
- De-clip
- De-crackle
- De-ess
- De-hum
- De-plosive
- De-reverb
- De-rustle
- De-wind
- Deconstruct
- Dialogue Isolate with De-reverb
- Dialogue Contour
- Dither
- EQ
- EQ Match
- Fade
- Gain

- Guitar De-noise
- Interpolate
- Leveler
- Loudness Control
- Loudness Optimize
- Mixing
- Mouth De-click
- Music Rebalance
- Normalize
- Phase
- Repair Assistant
- Resample
- Signal Generator
- Spectral De-noise
- Spectral Recovery
- Spectral Repair
- Streaming Preview
- Time & Pitch
- Variable Pitch
- Variable Time
- Voice De-noise
- Wow & Flutter

Pricing: RX 11 Advanced costs €844.35

By utilizing RX 11's advanced modules, audio professionals can address a wide range of issues in their recordings, from removing unwanted noises to isolating vocals and instruments. Its comprehensive set of tools makes it an indispensable asset for anyone serious about audio restoration and enhancement.

6 Mixing with AI

Automated Tools for Music Production

To produce a successful or good song today, we need audio effects both on individual tracks or instruments and on the stereo master. This involves mixing, where each track is adjusted so that the overall mix sounds as good as possible, and mastering, where the stereo master—that is, the entire music production—is processed to sound just as full as the latest track by David Guetta or another successful production.

Digital Audio Workstations (DAWs) offer numerous audio effects that are now of extremely high quality. These effects are often integrated via plugin interfaces like VST to use audio effects from external manufacturers. Companies like Waves, Universal Audio, and Soundtoys have established themselves in this field. In this chapter, I will first give you a brief overview of the common audio effects used in a production today before I delve into tools that employ artificial intelligence to simplify the setup of these effects.

Common Audio Effects

Dynamic Processors

Dynamics are essential for controlling the volume of a signal. Imagine recording a singer who sings very softly in the verse and extremely loudly in the chorus. This could pose a problem because not every listening environment can handle a wide dynamic range. If we listen to this song in the car, for example, we'd have to set the overall volume so that either the chorus is too loud or the verse is too quiet. This is where the compressor comes into play: it reduces the volume of everything that is louder than a certain point (threshold). The ratio, which can be set to 2:1, 4:1, or higher, determines how strongly the signal is compressed. A limiter, on the other hand, limits the volume to a maximum level by heavily reducing everything that exceeds the threshold. With an expander or a noise gate, quiet passages can be made even quieter or completely suppressed.

DOI: 10.4324/9781003621126-6

Equalizers

Everything we hear is divided into frequencies. A newborn person hears from 20 Hertz up to about 20,000 kilohertz. As we age, our ability to hear high frequencies decreases. The human voice starts at about 150 Hertz (male) or 250 Hertz (female) and reaches up to 12,000 kilohertz. With an equalizer, we can adjust these frequencies. A parametric EQ allows us to boost or attenuate specific frequencies, while a shelf EQ uniformly raises or lowers all frequencies above or below a certain point. Filters are used to cut off high or low frequencies.

Delay

A delay, also known as an echo, repeats the input signal after a certain time. In music production, this effect is often used rhythmically so that the repetitions occur in sync with the song's tempo.

Reverb

Reverb simulates the natural reverberation of a space. In a room with bare walls, like a garage or a church, we hear many echoes that blend into a wash of sound. This effect gives tracks depth and a sense of space.

Modulation Effects

Modulation effects like chorus, flanger, and phaser add movement and interesting timbres to the audio signal.

Distortion

Distortion effects like distortion, saturation, and amp simulation are particularly important in music styles like rock, metal, and hardcore. They give the sound aggressiveness and character.

You typically apply several of these effects to each instrument, each drum in the drum kit, and each vocal track. It takes experience and practice to know which effects to choose and how to set them optimally.

AI-Based Tools for Mixing

That's why there are tools like the Pure Bundle, Neutron 5 by iZotope, and several others that help us find the optimal settings. These AI-based tools analyze the audio signal and either automatically make the best settings or offer effects that were not possible without AI before. Today, it's possible to use a single command to reduce the breathing noises in a vocal or speech recording, lessen the sliding noises on a guitar, and detect and minimize various unwanted sounds.

A process that has become extremely important and is now offered by many manufacturers is the separation of music into individual tracks. You can upload a complete song into these tools and usually receive four separate audio files: one for the drums, one for the vocals, one for the bass, and one for everything else. The quality of these tools has significantly improved in recent years and is now very impressive.

In this chapter, I will provide you with an overview of the most important tools and wish you a lot of fun exploring them.

By incorporating these advanced tools into your workflow, you can enhance your music production process, achieve professional-quality mixes, and unlock new creative possibilities with the help of artificial intelligence.

Pure Bundle

The Pure Bundle by Sonible consists of a series of audio plugins where the user benefits from AI-assisted functions to find the right settings. So if you're using a music production program like Logic Pro, Ableton Live, or similar, you can load as many of these plugins onto any track as you like. The bundle includes an equalizer, a compressor, a limiter, a reverb, and a plugin called Pure:Unmask.

Pure:EQ

An equalizer is used to boost or attenuate specific frequency ranges. Often, my subscribers on YouTube ask me, "What is the best setting for an equalizer?" The problem is that this setting can vary greatly. The sound depends on the singer, the microphone used, the room acoustics, and the distance or position relative to the microphone. It requires some practical experience to hear which frequency ranges should be adjusted with an EQ.

The user interface of Pure:EQ makes it very easy even for less experienced users. First, you select the type of audio signal from a menu—whether it's a guitar, a bass drum, or vocals. Then you press the Learn button and start playback. The AI now analyzes the audio signal and calculates an equalizer curve. With the Balance function, you can set the intensity of the desired effect, where "0" means no change and "100" means maximum change. The Style function allows you to select different types like Bright, Warm, and Neutral. The Dynamic slider lets you choose whether the curve remains static or dynamically adapts to the incoming audio signal.

Pure:Comp

A compressor is used to reduce the dynamic range of an audio signal. This can be easily explained with an example. Let's say Lady Gaga has just recorded a vocal track for a new ballad. In the verse, she sings very softly and gently, while in the chorus, she sings with full power. If we set the vocal volume so that it doesn't clip in the chorus, the verse will be barely audible in quiet passages, especially when the song is played on a device like a car radio or a smart speaker with ambient noise. The differences between loud and quiet passages are simply too great.

This is where a compressor comes into play: it reduces the volume of signals that are louder than a threshold defined by the user. In this way, the dynamic range of the signal is reduced, and the quiet passages become louder without the loud passages clipping.

The user interface of Pure:Comp is designed to make settings as easy as possible for the user. Similar to the EQ, the user selects the type of audio signal—such as vocals, drums, or bass—from a menu. Then, the user presses the Learn button, starts playback, and waits a few seconds while the AI analyzes the audio signal. After that, only a few controls are available to adjust the desired effect. With the Compression slider, you can set the intensity of the effect, where 0 means no change and 100 means maximum change. Through the Style setting, various sound options are available:

- Clean for a transparent sound
- Dirty for a warmer compression character
- Mixed, a blend of the two

The Clarity setting allows you to further increase transparency.

Pure:Verb

A reverb, also known as hall, is created by a multitude of reflections or delays perceived as room acoustics. This can range from a short and warm sound in a small living room to a large and metallic sound in a church. A classic reverb offers many setting options for the desired sound besides the main parameters like Amount (Wet) and Size.

Similar to other plugins in this series, you select the type of incoming audio signal, press the Learn button, and play the audio to the AI. After a short analysis, you already hear the room sound calculated by the AI and can regulate the intensity of the reverb effect with the Mix slider and adjust the length with the Size slider. Additionally, there's the Synthetic slider to control the amount of synthetic elements, as well as the Mode slider. The latter is particularly important because it can set different types of room sounds:

- Normal: The typical reverb as expected.
- Reverse: This special effect setting makes the reverb sound backward.
- Bounce: Creates exciting rhythmic patterns.

Pure:Limit

A limiter, comparable to a compressor, regulates the dynamic range of the audio signal but specifically focuses on limiting peaks in the signal. This serves to protect against clipping and is often used as the last effect on the stereo master to ensure consistent levels. With Pure:Limit, the adjustment process is simplified: after selecting the music style like Rock, R&B, etc., you press the Learn button and wait for the AI analysis. Then you regulate the desired volume level with the dB Gain, thereby adjusting the compression. A higher setting of the Gain slider enhances the limiter's action accordingly. A limiter set too aggressively can cause unwanted pumping or distortion. The Style setting allows you to adjust the processing between Hard and Soft, while Inflate influences the level and energy of the bass components of the signal.

Pure:Unmask

This plugin, which has become one of my favorites when producing my podcast, takes a slightly different approach. In my podcast, there are regularly places where music plays underneath my narration. In the past, I simply reduced the volume of the music significantly to make the speech easily understandable. Now, I use Pure:Unmask on the music track and send my speech into the plugin's sidechain—a secondary input that controls the processing of the audio signal. Whenever my speech enters the plugin via the sidechain, the frequencies of my voice are reduced in the music. This allows me to keep the music slightly louder; you hear more of the music but understand the speech even better. Technically speaking, Pure:Unmask uses spectral unmasking to prevent frequency spectrum interferences between two tracks, ensuring clarity in the audio.

Applying the Plugin Is Simple

1. Place it on the track you want to reduce dependent on a control signal—in my example, the music.
2. Send the control signal—in my case, the speech—into the sidechain input. This works slightly differently in each program, but don't worry; the plugin provides a link to a webpage that offers detailed instructions for every common program.
3. After selecting the sidechain profile in the menu, such as vocals or guitar, and pressing the Learn button, you can start playback.
4. Within a few seconds, the plugin learns enough and begins to reduce the frequencies of the main audio signal.

The strength of this reduction is controlled by the Unmasking slider, where 0 leaves the signal unchanged and 100 produces the maximum change.

The Resolution setting allows you to control the level of detail in the plugin's frequency analysis. A higher resolution takes more nuances into account and results in a more subtle effect. Speed, on the other hand, adjusts the response time of the reduction process, similar to the attack and release times of a conventional compressor. Lower speed values lead to a smoother overall reduction, while higher values ensure that Pure:Unmask also reduces the levels of short transient signals.

Pure:Unmask is typically used to ensure that a speaker or singer is easily understood over music. However, the plugin can also be used to help lead instruments or drums stand out better against the background.

Pricing

The Pure Bundle currently costs €99, but you can also purchase the plugins individually:

- Pure:EQ—€29
- Pure:Unmask—€29
- Pure:Comp—€29
- Pure:Limit—€29
- Pure:Reverb—€65

By integrating the Pure Bundle into your workflow, you can leverage AI technology to simplify complex mixing tasks, achieve professional sound quality, and focus more on the creative aspects of music production.

Neutron 5 Takes Over Mixing Your Track

One of the most important steps in producing a song is mixing. In this process, the correct volume is set for each track or instrument. The individual instruments are positioned in the stereo panorama—that is, whether they are heard more from the left or right speaker—and each track is checked for dynamics, sound quality, and spatial depth. Audio effects are applied to the individual tracks, providing functions like equalizer, compressor, delay, reverb, distortion, modulation, and much more. The goal of a mix is to achieve a balanced overall sound where each instrument or track finds its position in the mix. Often, the best professionals are hired for this process because it determines how the final song will sound.

The company iZotope has developed the plugin Neutron—a small piece of software that can be loaded onto any track in any music program to optimize the sound of that track and improve the overall mix. Neutron uses artificial intelligence to analyze and then optimize the sound of each track. Using it is incredibly simple:

1 Load Neutron onto the desired track:
  Open the plugin in your DAW and load Neutron onto the track you want to process.

2. Activate Assistant View:
   At the top center of the plugin, you'll find two buttons. Press the left button labeled "Assistant View" and start playback. Neutron will now analyze the audio material of this track and begin optimizing the sound with its internal audio effects.
3. Display Detailed View:
   After the analysis is complete, you can switch back to the "Detailed View" button at the top to see which audio effects Neutron has loaded and what settings have been made.

Creating the Overall Mix

As previously mentioned, it is also possible to create an overall mix where the volumes and panorama positions for all tracks are set. To do this, proceed as follows:

1. Load Neutron Visual Mixer onto the stereo master:
   Load the plugin "Neutron Visual Mixer" into the master track of your project.
2. Load Neutron 5 onto all individual tracks or groups:
   Load Neutron 5 onto all individual tracks or groups that you want to include in the mix.
3. Start Mix Assistant:
   Start the Mix Assistant and playback of the song. Neutron 5 analyzes the volumes and begins making the corresponding adjustments.

Personal Impressions

In my tests, I was very impressed with how Neutron 5 was able to optimize the sound of many instruments. However, the idea of having the entire song mixed by artificial intelligence did not convince me. But that may be because I have been producing music for over 30 years and know exactly what I want.

Conclusion

Neutron 5 by iZotope is a powerful tool that can help both beginners and experienced producers improve their mixes. By using artificial intelligence, the mixing process is accelerated and simplified, while the results still sound professional. Whether you ultimately leave the entire mix to the AI or only certain tasks is up to you.

Price: Neutron 5 (Change Edition) costs €188.30

See Neutron in Action

https://youtu.be/nyo6nUVfevk?si=wDffZT52PfiyVdTp&t=264

RipX by Hit'n'Mix

RipX DAW—A Revolution in Music Production

RipX DAW by Hit'n'Mix is software that reimagines music production entirely. Unlike traditional DAWs, RipX DAW allows you to import your own stereo audio files directly into the program window. Immediately upon import, the track is analyzed, starting with the tempo. A timeline is created, similar to conventional DAWs, but here, the entire audio is displayed in a piano roll based on pitch.

The various elements of the track—such as vocals, drums, bass, and chordal instruments—are indicated by different colors. This enables you to instantly engage and change or edit any note. On the left side of the program, you have access to the individual groups. By clicking on the respective name—for example, "Voice"—you select the vocals. On the right, a multitude of effects appears that can be applied solely to the selected group.

A standout feature is the "Harmony" function. As soon as you click on "Harmony," a second and third voice are automatically added to the lead vocal, a third above and a third below. The interval can, of course, be adjusted. Additionally, the vocals can be adapted to a specific scale. This makes it possible to transform the vocals of a song sung in major to minor with just a few clicks. Classic effects like compressor, chorus, and delay are also available.

Another remarkable function is the ability to replace any instrument with another. You can select the entire vocals by clicking on "Voice" or choose individual notes of the vocals. In the "Sounds" menu on the right, you can then select an instrument, and the vocals are transformed into that instrument. For example, you can turn the vocals into a Stratocaster, marimbas, a harp, or any other instrument.

At first glance, RipX DAW appears to be the DAW of the future. Upon closer inspection, however, you realize that many functions you're familiar with from classic DAWs like Ableton, FL Studio, or Cubase are not available here in the usual quality. Therefore, RipX DAW may not be suitable as your primary music program. Thanks to the export function, however, it is possible to import audio files, extract the individual groups (stems) like drums, vocals, bass, etc., and then further process these audio files in another DAW like Ableton Live. MIDI files can also be exported, making RipX DAW an interesting addition to traditional DAWs.

This innovative software offers you a completely new approach to music production and opens up numerous creative possibilities that you won't find in conventional DAWs.

Price: RipX DAW costs €182 for the Pro version

See RipX in Action

https://youtu.be/nyo6nUVfevk?si=w4S2e00O5V8g6Nel&t=295

Separating Vocals and Instruments: Creating Stems with AI

The dream of many music producers to access the individual tracks of an existing song is as old as music production itself. Whether from YouTube, Spotify, or other sources—having vocals, drums, bass, or other instruments available separately has long been a challenge. These separate tracks are called stems. The most common stems typically include tracks for drums, bass, vocals, and the remaining instruments.

In the past, there was hardly a practical way to generate such stems from a finished song. Some tricks, like using an instrumental version to create an a cappella track, were available but usually offered limited results. However, this has fundamentally changed with the use of artificial intelligence. AI can learn from thousands of examples how the individual elements of a song—such as drums, bass, vocals, and other instruments—sound and can accordingly separate them from one another.

The results of these new AI-powered programs are astonishingly good, though not yet perfect. In the generated a cappella tracks, artifacts are often audible, and especially the reverberation shows that the separation between the individual tracks is not yet entirely successful. Nevertheless, the progress is impressive, and the technology is rapidly evolving.

The latest program to integrate this functionality is Logic Pro by Apple. In my assessment, Logic Pro currently delivers the highest quality results in stem separation. However, I recommend testing various tools yourself to find the solution that best suits your needs.

Here is a list of programs I've found that offer the ability to create stems using artificial intelligence:

Lalal.ai

Allows the separation of vocals, drums, bass, voice and noise, electric guitar, acoustic guitar, piano, synthesizer, strings, and wind instruments.

Fadr.com

Offers detailed separation options, such as splitting the drum track into individual elements like bass drum or snare drum.

RipX

A tool specializing in the separation and remastering of audio material.

iZotope RX11

An advanced audio repair software that provides AI-assisted tools for audio separation.

Logic Pro (Apple)

The latest program with this function, delivering the highest quality results in many tests.

See the Stems Splitter of Logic Pro in Action

https://youtu.be/nyo6nUVfevk?si=-0ubrcfUGR6muxMR&t=337

Musicfy

Another tool that enables the creation of stems using artificial intelligence, characterized by a user-friendly interface and high separation quality.

Important Note

When using these tools, always ensure that you have the legal rights to process and manipulate the audio material. Unauthorized use of copyrighted material may infringe upon copyright laws.

By leveraging these innovative tools, music producers and enthusiasts can explore new creative possibilities in remixing, sampling, and reimagining existing songs. The ability to separate individual elements of a track opens up opportunities that were previously difficult or impossible to achieve.

7 The Evolution of the Musician

The Future of Sound Generation and Composition

In the 1960s and 1970s, music production primarily consisted of recordings of musicians playing real instruments—often simultaneously, in a single room. The Beatles were among the first to experiment with multi-track recording, allowing individual instruments to be recorded one after the other. This technique enabled a more nuanced editing of each track and fundamentally revolutionized music production.

Today, the most common method for recording instruments is working with digital music programs, known as DAWs (Digital Audio Workstations). In this process, virtual instruments are recorded onto instrument or MIDI tracks. Musicians load a sound into the program and play the desired melody or accompaniment either via a MIDI keyboard or by directly inputting the notes into the DAW's piano roll. The latter technique has become especially popular among DJs. It's impressive to see how quickly experienced users can insert notes into the piano roll—the result is often more precise and perfect than what could be recorded live on a keyboard.

For sound design, essentially two techniques are available: sampling and synthesis. Both sound categories are already integrated into most DAWs. Sampling technology uses recordings of real instruments, while synthesizers generate sounds electronically. Apple's Logic Pro DAW offers an especially wide selection of sampled sounds, such as strings, brass, pianos, and basses, as well as a broad range of synthesizer sounds. Additionally, the program allows the use of external VST plugins, enabling musicians to access nearly unlimited additional sounds and effects.

One of the most popular VST plugins in the sampling domain is Kontakt by Native Instruments, which stands out with its comprehensive collection of sounds. Companies like Vienna Symphonic Library, Orchestral Tools, and Spitfire Audio have specialized in offering high-quality orchestral sounds. These libraries consist of extensive recordings of real instruments, mapped onto a keyboard so they can be played in real time. The variety ranges from staccato and legato to pizzicato and many other playing techniques.

The market now also boasts an impressive variety of piano sounds. For example, Native Instruments sampled Alicia Keys' piano note by note at various

DOI: 10.4324/9781003621126-7

volume levels. Similarly, the company developed an impressive piano sound named Noire, recorded in Hall 3 of the Funkhaus Berlin with numerous microphones. There are also specialized plugins for guitars—both acoustic and electric—that convincingly simulate typical playing styles to the point where they are hardly distinguishable from real recordings.

Of course, there are also numerous companies that specialize in simulating real drums, offering high-quality sounds and plugins. Leading developers include:

- Toontrack with Superior Drummer 3, one of the most comprehensive and realistic drum plugins on the market.
- XLN Audio with Addictive Drums 2, offering a wide range of versatile drum kits and styles.
- Steven Slate Digital with Steven Slate Drums 5, known for its excellent sounds and flexible customization options.
- Native Instruments with the Abbey Road Drummer Series, capturing the sonic aesthetics of various musical eras.
- BFD Drums with BFD3, which impresses with its natural sounds and extensive processing options.

These plugins allow the simulation of a wide array of drum sounds in the highest quality, from classic acoustic drums to modern, genre-specific sounds, providing music producers with an enormous range of creative possibilities.

In the realm of synthesizers, there is a multitude of plugins that emulate various models. Serum by Xfer Records has become particularly established, although new synthesizers continue to emerge, surprising users with innovative approaches. An example of this is The Legend HZ by Synapse Audio, backed by none other than the famous film composer Hans Zimmer. He has recreated his analog synthesizers, housed in his studio, as plugins to make the impressive sound capabilities available digitally.

Choosing the right sound for a music production remains a challenge. Either you master the sound capabilities of a synthesizer perfectly and can program the desired sound yourself, or you have to sift through numerous presets until you find the ideal sound. This is where artificial intelligence comes into play, creating new approaches to find or even generate sounds faster. AI also increasingly facilitates the process of inputting notes, enabling the creation of convincing compositions even without in-depth knowledge of music theory.

The evolution of the musician has shifted from working with acoustic instruments to a virtual, software-supported creativity where modern technologies like artificial intelligence are becoming increasingly important. Today, many musicians operate in the tension between traditional craftsmanship and digital innovation—a dynamic that is sustainably transforming music production and opening up new creative possibilities.

By embracing these advancements, musicians and producers can navigate the ever-evolving landscape of music production, leveraging both traditional techniques and cutting-edge technologies to create innovative and high-quality music.

Emergent Drums

AI Generates New Drum Sounds

Choosing the right drum sounds is crucial for the quality of a club track or a pop song. It's not just about using the same sounds as everyone else but about creating your own unique drum sounds. This can be achieved by programming synthesizers, mixing multiple existing drum samples, and applying audio effects, which is often very time-consuming.

With Emergent Drums, it's possible to generate new drum sounds with just one click. You can either select a sound from the internal library or drag an audio file from your hard drive into one of the 16 slots of the internal drum sampler. Then, using a fader, you can set whether the new sound should be more "Similar" or "Random" (thus significantly different). A single click is enough, and you already have a new sound generated by AI.

This tool significantly eases the work of producers creating drum libraries. You can place each existing sample on all 16 slots using the copy/paste function and create 16 variations with just one click using the "Regenerate All Drum Pads" function.

Emergent Drums costs $49.

See Emergent Drums in Action

https://youtu.be/nyo6nUVfevk?si=Cq2rxgIHAARV4qMY&t=387

XO by XLN Audio

The Ultimate Solution for Selecting Drum Samples

For music producers, finding the perfect drum samples is often a challenge. Despite extensive sample libraries, identifying the optimal drum sample—whether it's the right kick, the appropriate snare, or other elements—remains difficult. This is where XO comes into play. This plugin analyzes all drum samples on your hard drive and organizes them into an interactive 3D landscape reminiscent of the universe. Each sample is represented as a point, with the color indicating its respective category. For example, kick drums are red, snares are blue, and hi-hats are yellow. By zooming and navigating through this landscape, you can effortlessly find the desired samples. Similar sounds are positioned close to each other, significantly simplifying the search for the perfect sample.

But XO offers more than just an intuitive selection of drum samples. It also functions as a fully-fledged drum machine, allowing you to assign samples to pads and program complete drum beats. Additionally, numerous effects are available to refine and personalize your sounds.

With XO, searching for the right drum samples becomes an inspiring and efficient experience that boosts your productivity and sparks your creativity.

XO costs €129.

Logic Pro 11

Your Virtual Band Member: The AI Session Player

Logic Pro by Apple is considered one of the most popular music programs in the professional realm. In May 2024, Apple introduced Version 11, which integrates several functions that utilize artificial intelligence. One of the most remarkable new features is the Session Player, which consists of three virtual musicians: a drummer, a bassist, and a keyboard player.

Features of the Session Player

Easy Creation of Music Phrases

Automated Music Phrases

Simply create a track, and an eight-bar music phrase is instantly generated.

Intuitive Control

With sliders like "Complexity" and "Intensity," as well as by clicking within a graphical user interface, you can precisely influence what these musicians play.

Integration with Chord Tracks

Harmonic Adjustment

The bassist and keyboard player reference a chord track where you can input the chords of your composition. This ensures that the generated phrases harmoniously align with your music.

MIDI Export

Flexible Editing

Generated Music Performances

The generated music performances can be converted into MIDI. This allows you to further edit and adjust the notes on-screen to achieve your desired result.

Advantages of Using the Session Player

In practice, experienced musicians who also play the piano might sometimes dismiss the new Session Players as mere novelties. However, DJs who are less proficient in piano playing greatly appreciate this functionality. By inputting the chords, they can determine what music the Session Players should perform through simple settings. This makes music production accessible even for less experienced musicians and allows for quicker realization of their creative ideas.

How to Create a Drum Track with the Session Players

1 Open the Track Menu and Select "New Tracks…":
Navigate to the track menu and choose to create new tracks.
2 Select the Session Drummer from the "Session Player" Category and Confirm with "Create":
Choose the Session Drummer option and confirm its creation.
3 Logic Automatically Creates an Eight-Bar Region Ready for Adjustments:
An eight-bar region is generated, ready for you to make adjustments.
4 Choose the Desired Style by Clicking on the Drum Graphic (e.g., Pop Rock, Retro Rock, Hard Rock, etc.):
Select the drum style that best fits your project.
5 Fine-Tune with the Sliders for Complexity and Intensity:
Adjust the complexity and intensity sliders to shape the drum performance.
6 Adjust the Details of Your Drum Performance in the Main Area of the Session Player:
Make further refinements to the drum performance in the main interface.
7 Choose from Various Presets for Kick and Snare:
Select different presets to customize the kick and snare sounds.
8 Choose Between Hi-Hat, Cymbals, or Tom:
Decide which hi-hat or cymbal sounds to incorporate.

9. Refine Fills, Swing, and Dynamics:
   Tweak the fills, swing feel, and dynamic range of the drums.
10. Select the "Details" Section for Further Adjustments:
   Access additional settings for more precise control.
11. Add Ghost Notes to Give the Beat Additional Grooves:
   Incorporate ghost notes to enhance the groove of the beat.
12. Use the Snare Menu for Precise Playing Styles Like Rim Shot or Side Stick:
   Customize snare hits for different playing techniques.
13. Add Percussive Elements Like Tambourine or Shaker:
   Enhance the rhythm with additional percussive elements.
14. Control Nuances Like Hi-Hat Opening and Dynamics:
   Adjust the opening of the hi-hat and overall dynamics.
15. Select "Manual" to Program a Basic Rhythm with a Simple

Step Sequencer Based on the Beat Created by Logic

Manually program rhythms using the step sequencer for more customized beats.

How to Create a Bass Track with the Session Players

1. Open the Track Menu and Select "New Tracks…":
   Navigate to the track menu and choose to create new tracks.
2. Select the Session Bass from the "Session Player"
   Category and Confirm with "Create":
   Choose the Session Bass option and confirm its creation.
3. Logic Automatically Creates an Eight-Bar Region Ready for Adjustments:
   An eight-bar region is generated, ready for you to make adjustments.
4. Below the Tempo Display is the Chord Track,
   Where Logic Pro Automatically Generates a Few Chords for the Bassist to Respond To:
   Logic Pro creates a chord progression that the bassist will follow.
5. To the Left of This Chord Track is the "Toggle Global Tracks"
   Switch, Allowing You to Open the Chord Track View:
   Use the toggle switch to view and edit the chord track.
6. Double-Click on the Chords to Edit Them:
   Modify the chords as needed for your composition.
7. When the Pattern is Active, the Session Player Appears Below:
   The Session Player interface becomes visible when the pattern is active.
8. Choose the Desired Style by Clicking on the Bass Graphic
   (e.g., Pop Rock, Retro Rock, Pop Songwriter, etc.):
   Select the bass style that fits your track.

9 Fine-Tune with the Sliders for Complexity and Intensity:
Adjust the complexity and intensity sliders to shape the bass performance.
10 Adjust the Details of Your Bass Performance in the Main Area of the Session Player:
Make further refinements to the bass performance in the main interface.
11 Choose a Preset for the Rhythm:
Select a preset that defines the rhythmic pattern of the bass.
12 Decide How Much Melody, Octaves, and Phrasing the Bass Should Play:
Customize the melodic elements, octave range, and phrasing of the bass.
13 Choose the Lowest Note the Bass Should Play:
Set the lowest note to define the bass's range.
14 Refine Fills, Swing, and Dynamics:
Tweak the fills, swing feel, and dynamic range of the bass.
15 Select the "Details" Section for Further Adjustments:
Access additional settings for more precise control.
16 Add Dead Notes to Give the Beat Additional Grooves:
Incorporate dead notes to enhance the groove of the beat.
17 Use the Snare Menu for Precise Playing Styles Like Rim Shot or Side Stick:
Customize snare hits for different playing techniques.
18 Add Percussive Elements Like Tambourine or Shaker:
Enhance the rhythm with additional percussive elements.
19 Control Nuances Like Hi-Hat Opening and Dynamics:
Adjust the opening of the hi-hat and overall dynamics.
20 Select "Manual" to Program a Basic Rhythm with a Simple Step Sequencer Based on the Beat Created by Logic:
Manually program rhythms using the step sequencer for more customized beats.

Pricing

Logic Pro 11 costs €229.99.

See the Session Player of Logic Pro in Action

https://youtu.be/nyo6nUVfevk?si=cG1hZyXqUmlXu3Yt&t=427

Synplant 2

AI Programs Your Synthesizer

The best sound provider in music production remains the synthesizer. Compared to other instruments, it offers the ability to alter sounds endlessly and vary them through automation throughout a song. However, programming a

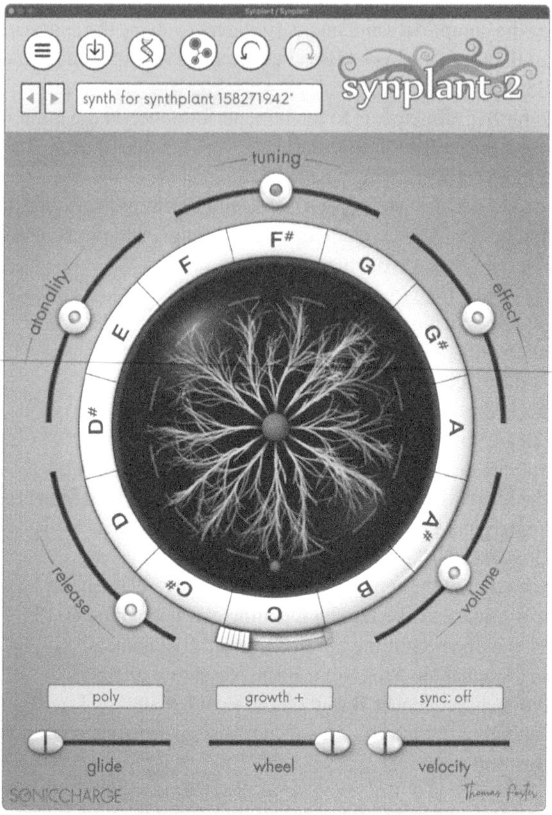

Figure 7.1 Synplant 2's Interface, an AI-driven Synthesizer by Sonic Charge.

synthesizer to achieve the desired sound is not easy. Even if you have familiarized yourself with every function of the synthesizer and understand exactly what each knob does, it still requires a lot of experience.

Sonic Charge recognized this problem and developed the first synthesizer that can program itself using artificial intelligence based on a reference sample. You simply upload an audio file that contains the desired synthesizer sound, and the AI then attempts to adjust the synthesizer's knobs to resemble the reference sound.

How It Works

1 Click on "Genopatch (Sample To Patch)":
  This is the fourth button at the very top.

2 Click on "Load Reference Sound":
This is the first button at the bottom left.
3 Choose a Sample (Reference Sound) from Your Hard Drive:
Select the audio file you want to use as a reference.
4 Click on the First "Restart (ALT: Evolve From Patch)":
This is the left button among the four buttons with a double arrow.
5 Wait for Synplant 2 to Complete Its Calculations:
Allow the AI to process the reference sound.
6 Select the Best Result:
Each point that appears in the main display represents an attempt to program a sound according to your specifications. Click on the points and choose the best result.

Pricing

Synplant 2 costs €149.

See Synplant 2 in Action

https://youtu.be/nyo6nUVfevk?si=SMYicZLo-7QG8eMn&t=493

Captain Plugins

AI-Assisted Composition for Today's Musicians

As someone who has studied music and delved deeply into the world of music theory and practice from a young age, I have a clear idea of how music is "properly" composed. I learned to play the piano as a child, later my sister showed me the first chords on the guitar, and finally, I deepened my knowledge at the Mozarteum, where I learned classical music theory from the ground up. However, in the early 2000s, I experienced a revelation in Ibiza: DJs who had never played an instrument or studied music theory were producing tracks that often broke the rules but sounded incredibly refreshing and innovative. Their intuitive approach to music stood in stark contrast to my academic method, and yet they created something that was often more impressive and cooler than what I could produce with all my knowledge.

This experience made me realize that in music, it's not just theoretical knowledge that matters, but above all, the sense of sound and emotion. Many people today who produce music in a DAW do not have the classical musical education that I enjoyed. Nevertheless, they want to create high-quality music, and this is precisely where tools like Captain Plugins by Mixed In Key come into play. These plugins fill a crucial market gap: they offer support for those who want to compensate for their lack of theoretical knowledge and still achieve professional results.

The Captain Plugins are a suite of five tools that cover various aspects of music production. With Captain Chords, users can create chord progressions for different parts of a song, such as verses and choruses. Captain Deep generates corresponding basslines, automatically taking over the chords from Captain Chords. Similarly, Captain Melody finds melodies that perfectly match the chords. Captain Beat specializes in creating rhythmic beats for different music styles, and Captain Play allows you to play using a MIDI keyboard or your computer keyboard, with the correct scales and chords automatically set.

Each of these plugins also offers internal sounds that can be used directly. Alternatively, the generated MIDI files can be exported to the DAW to work further with other, possibly higher-quality plugins.

These tools also enable non-music theorists to make music creatively and intuitively without having to compromise on professional results. Captain Plugins are the perfect proof that artificial intelligence can expand the creative potential of every musician.

Quick Start Guide to Using Captain Plugins

1 Load Captain Chords:

- Create a new track in your DAW and load the Captain Chords plugin.
- At the top left, set the desired key and scale in Key & Scale.
- Click directly below on Chord Progression, which will bring up three menus in the middle top.
- In the first menu, Banks, you can filter by music style.
- In the second menu, choose the type of chord progression you want.
- In the third menu, select a specific chord sequence, typically spanning four measures.
- Now, go to the Rhythm menu on the left and select a rhythm pattern for how the chords should be played.
- Further down, find the Sound Preset menu where you can choose a sound, such as a piano or synthesizer, for the chords.

2 Load Captain Deep:

- Create a new track and load the Captain Deep plugin.
- The previously created chords are automatically recognized, and a suitable bass is generated.
- In the Rhythm menu on the left, you can change the bass rhythm.
- Select an appropriate bass sound under Sound Preset.

3 Load Captain Beat:

- Load the Captain Beat plugin on another track.
- In the left menu, select a suitable Pattern.
- Under Drum Kit, choose the desired sounds for the beat.

4 Load Captain Melody:

- Create another track and load Captain Melody.
- The chords from Captain Chords are automatically recognized here as well.
- In the main window, where notes are already displayed, click the centered Plus sign on the left to generate an initial melody.
- Adjust the melody further using the menus and switches at the top.
- Change the sound in the Sound Preset menu on the left side.

5 Export MIDI and Audio:

- In each plugin, you will find three squares on the right side. The rightmost square is labeled Export MIDI.
- Hold down the mouse button, drag the square to a new track in your DAW to export the notes as a MIDI file.
- Alternatively, use the Render Audio function to create an audio file that you can further edit in your DAW.
- With this quick start, you can fully utilize the Captain Plugins Epic series and create professional music tracks in no time.

Captain Plugins Epic costs €99.

Musicfy

Your Voice Becomes an Instrument

A fascinating way to create new sounds is offered by the AI platform Musicfy, which allows transforming the human voice into various instruments. On the Musicfy website, you can upload your own voice and convert it into a wide range of instruments, including electric guitar, drums, violin, trumpet, or the exotic Indian shehnai. This technology opens up new creative avenues for musicians and producers, enabling the creation of sounds that are difficult to achieve through traditional methods.

The success of the transformation heavily depends on how well the singer can vocally mimic the playing style of the desired instrument. During my experiments with the platform, I managed to modulate my voice so that it sounded astonishingly authentic, resembling a jazz trumpet—often more convincing than traditional sample instruments. Similarly, you can beatbox and transform these recordings into drum sounds. The result is not always realistic, but that is part of the charm of this technique. You obtain sounds that are fresh and new, and these experimental results can be used in music productions as unique timbres that have never been heard before.

In addition to transforming voices into instruments, Musicfy offers the ability to change your voice into those of well-known personalities like Bruno

Mars, Donald Trump, or Billie Eilish. You can also generate short loops from text prompts that can be directly used in music productions. However, I was particularly impressed by the ability to create new instrumental sounds from vocals. This method gives musicians an additional dimension of creativity that goes far beyond conventional sample libraries.

Musicfy also allows users to fully commercially utilize the generated sounds. This means that you own both the mechanical and recording rights to the created sounds, which is especially important for producers who want to release their music. The platform is easy to use, but you should ensure to use as dry a cappellas as possible without reverb or background noise to achieve the best results. Overall, Musicfy represents a revolutionary way to create music in entirely new ways. The combination of AI and human creativity creates soundscapes that are not only unusual but often surprisingly inspiring.

Synth GPT

Generate Synthesizer Sounds with a Text Prompt

A highly fascinating concept is a plugin by Fadr.com called SynthGPT. With this plugin, you simply enter a text prompt, for example, "Mallet Bell," and based on this text prompt, one hundred different presets or sounds are generated, which you can listen to and play via the keyboard. Since I find this concept incredibly exciting, I contacted Fadr multiple times, but unfortunately, I have not received a response to date. Therefore, I was unable to test this tool, which is still in the beta phase, myself.

Instead, I had to rely on the tests of two YouTube colleagues who have already introduced SynthGPT in their videos: Ey Genn! and MMVMUZIC. Unfortunately, these videos show that the project is not yet mature. Often, the results do not meet expectations: in some cases, the audio sounds slightly damaged and exhibits clicks or popping noises. Additionally, the generated sounds are often not designed in a way that allows you to play a scale on a keyboard; instead, pressing a key frequently plays an entire chord or even a melody sequence.

Furthermore, it is not possible to edit the generated sounds afterwards. The options you are familiar with from other synthesizers—such as adjusting the sound through filters or envelopes—are completely missing here. You must accept the result as it is, or you cannot use it.

I watched both videos very closely, and unfortunately, the results did not convince me. However, the project is still in the beta phase, and I hope that it will be further improved in future versions.

Pricing

SynthGPT costs €149.

Figure 7.2 Advertisement Showcasing the Features of the Mugent Player.

8 AI in Mastering

Intelligent Tools for Professional Mastering

The final and crucial step of a music production is mastering. This process often takes place in specialized studios that receive the final mix of a song as a stereo file or as so-called stems—separate stereo files for different elements like drums, vocals, and bass. The goal of mastering is to optimize the mix so that it sounds perfect on the medium where it will be released, such as streaming platforms like Spotify. This involves adjusting volume, tonal balance, and dynamics so the song doesn't sound quieter or thinner than other tracks in playlists. Additionally, it's ensured that the song sounds good on all playback devices—from headphones and small speakers to large systems—in both stereo and mono.

In the past, songs were often sent to external mastering studios that specialized in this process. For particularly important productions, I occasionally sent my tracks to studios like MSM Munich[^1] or the Abbey Road Studios in London, which are still available today starting from £110 per song. However, in recent years, more and more musicians have begun mastering their songs themselves, not least for cost reasons. Often, this is done directly in the stereo output of the DAW (Digital Audio Workstation), which significantly simplifies the entire workflow.

The demand for user-friendly mastering solutions has led to more and more companies offering tools that support musicians in this process or even fully automate it. In this chapter, I'll give you an overview of the most important tools and show how artificial intelligence can be used in mastering to achieve the perfect sound. Enjoy!

Ozone: An Intelligent Mastering Tool for the Future

The company iZotope was one of the first to develop a plugin specifically for mastering. The first version of Ozone was released back in 2001 (Figure 8.1). Since then, iZotope has continuously added new modules to optimize sound quality and workflow for music producers and mastering engineers.

DOI: 10.4324/9781003621126-8

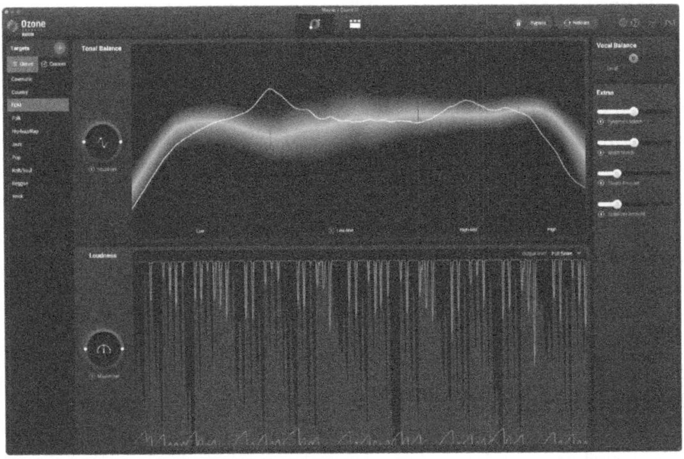

Figure 8.1 The Ozone 11 Interface, a Powerful Tool for Intelligent Mastering.

The current version of Ozone includes numerous modules that allow you to shape the sound of a master in a variety of ways. These include compressors and dynamics modules like Dynamics, Impact, Upward Compress, Vintage Compressor, and Vintage Limiter, which offer flexible dynamic processing. There are also various equalizer modules for fine-tuning the sound, such as Equalizer, Match EQ, Stabilizer, Low End Focus, and Vintage EQ.

Additionally, Ozone offers a module for editing the stereo width of a mix, the so-called Imager. With it, you can naturally expand or limit the stereo characteristics of the sound. Furthermore, there are other innovative modules like Clarity, Spectral Shaper, and Vintage Tape, which help refine the sound and give it the finishing touch.

In recent years, some new features have been added that are based on artificial intelligence. For example, Ozone offers the possibility to apply each of these modules not only to the entire stereo mix but specifically to the vocals, drums, or bass. This function opens up entirely new possibilities in the mastering process, as it allows you to edit the vocals in a finished stereo file differently from the drums, enabling very precise and creative work.

Another important innovation in Ozone is the Master Assistant, an AI-based assistant that helps the user find an optimal starting point for mastering. The Assistant analyzes the audio signal, automatically loads a selection of modules, and adjusts their settings based on the analyzed sound data. This is particularly helpful for users who do not have much experience in mastering and need guidance to quickly achieve a professional result.

Instructions for Using the Master Assistant in Ozone

To use the Master Assistant in Ozone, first place the Ozone plugin on the stereo output of your DAW (Digital Audio Workstation). Open the plugin and click on the red-blue button at the top center to start the Assistant. The software will then prompt you to play the loudest part of your mix. The Master Assistant analyzes the audio signal during playback and, after a few seconds, gives feedback with the words "Here is a great starting point."

After the Master Assistant has completed the analysis, it builds a processing chain that serves as a foundation for the further mastering process. You can now listen to the suggested settings and further refine them as desired until the desired result is achieved.

The Master Assistant also offers the possibility to access a library of predefined genre targets based on the analysis of current chart hits. Based on these genre targets, the Assistant automatically adjusts the tonal balance, vocal balance, width, dynamics, and loudness of the track to the target values of the selected songs. Advanced users can also create and save their own target curves based on reference tracks.

Overall, Ozone is a powerful tool for anyone who wants to make the mastering process efficient, whether through the use of intelligent assistants or through detailed control of every aspect of the sound.

Ozone 11 Costs

- €219 for the Full Version
- €439 for the Advanced Version

See Ozone 9 in Action

https://youtu.be/nyo6nUVfevk?si=BJMVF_rDCW6NUH5r&t=547

The Mastering Assistant in Logic Pro

Logic Pro is one of Apple's most popular music production programs. Since version 10.8, it offers the Mastering Assistant, an audio effect that you can apply to the stereo output of your audio production to optimize dynamics, stereo width, and sound. The Mastering Assistant automatically analyzes your project and applies corrective EQ, volume adjustments, and optimized stereo width as needed.

The Mastering Assistant provides a program-calculated equalizer curve to boost or cut individual frequencies. This curve is based on artificial intelligence and can be adjusted with a slider. At 0%, no processing is applied; at 100%, the maximum processing provided by the program is applied; and for more intensive processing, the slider can be increased up to 200%.

Personally, I'm not 100% convinced by the automatically calculated curve. Nevertheless, I find it very practical and user-friendly that Logic Pro makes a suggestion, allowing you to decide whether to apply this processing not at all, slightly, or extremely.

See the Mastering Assistant of Logic Pro in Action

https://youtu.be/nyo6nUVfevk?si=PmbosNrBBrFms6DA&t=602

LANDR: Automated Mastering as a Cost-Effective Alternative

For many musicians, mastering is a crucial step to successfully present their music on streaming platforms like Spotify, Apple Music, or Tidal. Professional mastering ensures that a track can hold its own sonically, even when played alongside hits from artists like David Guetta, Taylor Swift, or Ed Sheeran. However, professional mastering services are often expensive, and many independent artists shy away from the high costs that an experienced mastering engineer charges for their work. This is where LANDR comes into play—one of the most popular and cost-effective alternatives for automated mastering on the market.

LANDR offers a user-friendly platform that allows musicians to master their tracks quickly and easily. The process is straightforward: you upload your audio file to the LANDR homepage, and the artificial intelligence automatically analyzes the track. It considers various parameters like volume, dynamics, and frequency spectrum to create a master that brings out the best in the track.

Users can influence the sound of the mastering through two main parameters: Style and Loudness. The Style parameter offers three different options—Warm, Balanced, and Open—each emphasizing different sonic characteristics. "Warm" can make the sound warmer and fuller, while "Open" provides a wider, more transparent soundstage. "Balanced" offers an even combination of both styles and is suitable for most music genres.

The second parameter, Loudness, determines how loud the track will sound. There are three settings: Low, Medium, and High. "Low" is particularly suitable for genres like jazz or unplugged music, which prefer a more dynamic and natural playback. "Medium" is ideal for pop tracks that need to stand out on the radio or in playlists, while "High" is the best choice for EDM tracks that require high loudness and presence to convince in clubs or at festivals.

Another useful feature of LANDR is the ability to switch back and forth between the original and the mastered version. This allows users to directly compare the effects of different settings and adjust the mastering so that it perfectly achieves the desired sound. After a few clicks, you can download the finished master in various formats.

For musicians who want more control over the mastering process, LANDR also offers a premium option with a downloadable plugin that can be integrated directly into the DAW (Digital Audio Workstation). This plugin offers additional functions such as a parametric equalizer, controls for stereo width, a de-esser, an additional compressor, and finely tuned settings for loudness. Here, too, the options "Warm," "Balanced," and "Open" are available to precisely shape the sound.

The result is often astonishingly good—and in many cases significantly better than what many musicians have previously mastered themselves at home. While an experienced mastering engineer working in a perfect listening environment and understanding the fine nuances of a track remains the best option for achieving a truly outstanding master, the algorithms of AI-based mastering tools like LANDR are continuously improving. It is therefore possible that AI could even deliver better results than a traditional mastering engineer in the future.

LANDR Mastering Costs

Prices start at €15.99 per month
or €199.88 per year

9 AI in the DJ Booth

AI-Based Software for Innovative Mixing

How Artificial Intelligence is Revolutionizing DJ Programs and Redefining the Art of DJing.

The history of DJs begins in the 1940s when the first DJs hosted complete music programs on the radio. However, it wasn't until the 1960s that nightclubs, as we know them today, emerged—venues where records were played and rhythmic transitions between songs were attempted.

In the 1980s, the company Technics introduced a groundbreaking innovation with their turntables. These turntables, known as the Technics SL-1200, utilized a direct-drive motor where the platter was moved by a magnet. This patent allowed DJs to scratch and manually adjust the speed, which is essential for seamless and rhythmic transitions.

The 1990s saw the introduction of the first CD players for DJs, known as CDJs. These devices allowed DJs to use CDs in clubs, offering greater flexibility and new possibilities.

In the early 2000s, the first DJ software programs appeared, enabling mixing with computers. This software allowed extensive music libraries to be managed and offered features like automatic beatmatching, looping, and audio effects. DJs could bring their music on a USB stick, plug it into a CD player, and play and mix their tracks across multiple CD players and a mixer.

More recent DJ programs now even include samplers, allowing DJs to play individual drum elements or samples live over DJ hardware. They can also use a small step sequencer to program rhythms during a DJ set and integrate them into the performance. Native Instruments was one of the first companies to integrate stems into their DJ software. This function allows DJs to upload not just a single stereo file but up to four separate stereo tracks, enabling them to access vocals, drums, bass, and other elements independently.

A significant advancement came with the company Algoriddim and their software djay, which made it possible—with the help of artificial intelligence—to access individual tracks of a song in real-time. DJs can now upload a complete song and, during playback, mute the vocals or reduce the mix to drums and bass to create interesting transitions. This ability to isolate

DOI: 10.4324/9781003621126-9

specific elements like drums or vocals—not just turning down the bass as before—revolutionizes DJ capabilities.

Meanwhile, other companies have integrated these functions as well. Among the most well-known and popular DJ programs today, besides djay, are Traktor Pro 3 by Native Instruments, Serato DJ Pro, and Rekordbox. These software solutions each offer unique features that support DJs in their creative work:

- **djay Pro AI:** Known for its intuitive user interface and integration of AI stems, which allow real-time isolation of individual elements of a track. djay also offers comprehensive effects and integration with music streaming services like Tidal and SoundCloud.
- **Traktor Pro 4:** This software offers deep integration with hardware controllers and a variety of built-in effects. While Traktor doesn't offer real-time AI stems, it is possible to use pre-made stems to create creative mixes.
- **Serato DJ Pro:** Serato has made a name for itself through its stable performance and versatility. It supports Serato Stems, a technology for real-time isolation of audio tracks, and offers a wide range of effects as well as support for many controllers.
- **Rekordbox:** Developed by Pioneer, Rekordbox offers extensive DJ functions and support for Pioneer hardware. The software utilizes AI technologies to isolate vocals and other elements in real-time and offers comprehensive effects and streaming integrations.

These programs represent the current state of the art in DJ software and show how deeply artificial intelligence is now integrated into the art of DJing.

New programs like DJ Studio go even a step further by allowing a DJ set to be generated at the push of a button. The software analyzes key, tempo, and genre and tries virtually all conceivable combinations to guarantee the best transitions. The user receives a perfect DJ set that they can edit and modify as they wish. This opens up unprecedented possibilities for pre-produced DJ sets.

In this chapter, we will introduce the most important programs that support DJs with the help of artificial intelligence and explain the fantastic possibilities they offer. Enjoy!

Traktor Pro by Native Instruments

Traktor Pro 4 by Native Instruments is a comprehensive DJ software that offers a variety of features to professionally craft DJ sets. One of its standout features is the ability to switch the user interface between six different views. The "Essential" and "Extended" views are particularly recommended. The "Essential" view is a clear and simple version, ideal for beginners. For advanced users, the "Extended" view offers more functions and greater flexibility.

User Interface and Decks

At the top of the interface are two decks: Deck A on the left and Deck B on the right. These decks correspond to a CD player or turntable, into which songs can be loaded for playback. At the bottom is the browser where all songs are prepared for the DJ set.

Loading Songs into the Browser and Decks

To load a song into Traktor Pro's browser, simply drag it from your computer's Explorer into the browser. Once all the necessary songs are available in the browser, they can be dragged and dropped into the respective decks. Below each deck is a play button, which allows you to start the track with your mouse. For a professional DJ set, it's advisable to control as many actions as possible via a DJ controller, especially the rhythmic starting of tracks.

The Stems Function

A revolutionary feature of Traktor Pro is the Stems function, which allows you to isolate individual elements such as drums, vocals, and other instruments from any track. To use this function, you must first activate the "Generate Stems" feature. Right-click on the desired track in the browser and select "Generate Stems." This process takes about 1–2 minutes per song and generates four stereo files, which are stored in a new folder created by Traktor.

Working with Stems

After a song has been converted into stems, a new icon appears in the browser indicating that the song is now available as individual tracks. When you drag this song into a deck, the four stereo tracks—Drums, Bass, Other, and Vocals—are displayed. During playback, you can adjust the volume of individual tracks, mute or solo tracks, and add effects.

Revolutionary Mixing Techniques

This function enables a completely new way of mixing. For example, you can completely remove the drums from one track and start the drums of the next track, which are running in a loop. An a cappella of a previously played song can be introduced into the next track to connect the songs in an entirely new way. This opens up new creative possibilities and elevates DJing to a new level.

Conclusion

Traktor Pro 4 by Native Instruments offers an innovative platform for DJs to creatively and professionally craft their sets through its versatile functions and revolutionary Stems technology. Whether you're a beginner or a professional, the software provides the right tools for everyone to create impressive DJ sets.

Traktor Pro 4 costs €149

djay by Algoriddim—Pioneer of AI in DJing

The software djay by Algoriddim was the first DJ software to allow users to access individual elements of a song in real-time using artificial intelligence, such as vocals, drums, or other instruments. This functionality, known as "Neural Mix," has revolutionized the way DJs craft their sets.

A significant difference from other programs, particularly Traktor Pro 3 by Native Instruments, lies in how these programs handle stems—the individual audio tracks of a song. While with Traktor you need to convert the tracks in advance and save four separate stereo files on your hard drive to access them later, djay allows this editing without prior conversion. In djay, the DJ can immediately access the individual elements of a running stereo track, mute the vocals, isolate the drums, or apply effects to the remaining instruments—all in real-time.

This makes djay particularly flexible and intuitive, as no preparatory steps are required. Any song can be edited immediately after loading, allowing DJs to express their creativity in real-time and create spontaneous, dynamic sets.

Introduction to djay's User Interface

At the top right of djay's main window, there's a menu that allows you to switch between different views. To start, I recommend the "Extended" view. In this view, you see two decks at the top—Deck A on the left and Deck B on the right. Each deck essentially corresponds to a CD player or turntable on which tracks can be played and edited.

At the bottom is the browser, which offers a variety of options to organize the displayed content. Here, you can create your own playlists to organize your favorite songs clearly and access them quickly. A particularly useful feature is the ability to connect djay with various streaming platforms to play music directly from the cloud.

djay supports integration with several streaming services, including Apple Music, Tidal, SoundCloud, Beatport LINK, and Beatsource LINK. With Apple Music integration, available in 167 countries, djay users have access to over 100 million songs, including their personal library in iCloud. This direct connection allows DJs to integrate tracks into their sets in real-time without having to download music beforehand.

This seamless integration with various streaming services greatly expands your creative possibilities, allowing spontaneous access to a wide variety of tracks without needing to download the music first.

There are two ways to load tracks from the browser into the decks:

1. Right-click Method: Right-click on the desired song and select "Load on Deck 1."
2. Drag-and-Drop Method: Simply drag and drop the track into the desired deck.

Both decks have a Play button to start and stop the music.

To better orient yourself within the track, there's a waveform display of the entire song above the decks. This shows the entire progression of the track. Between the two decks, there's also a larger display that shows only the two to three bars currently being played. This facilitates timing and setting precise transitions.

At the beginning, I recommend activating the Sync buttons on both decks. This function automatically synchronizes the tempo of the two songs so that they run at the same tempo ("in time"). Many professional DJs claim that using the sync function is unprofessional, but it can definitely help beginners achieve good results more quickly.

Above the left deck are several buttons that open additional windows with more functions. These include:

- Loop Function: Allows you to repeat specific parts of a track.
- Effects Page: Here, various sound effects can be applied.
- Neural Mix Page: This function allows real-time isolation and editing of stems.
- Sampler Page: Here, short sound effects and loops can be played.

When you click on the third button, marked with a large "N" for "Neural Mix," an additional control panel with three faders opens between the browser and the two decks. These faders control the volume of the individual stems:

- Drums: Adjusts the volume of the drums.
- Harmonics: Controls the volume of all elements except drums and vocals.
- Vocals: Adjusts the volume of the vocals.

Above each fader, there's a "Solo" and a "Mute" button, allowing you to mute the drums or isolate only the vocals. These functions are extremely intuitive and easy to understand, making djay a particularly user-friendly software.

A particularly exciting feature I'd like to mention is the "Automix" function. To the right of the browser is the "Start Automix" button. Clicking this button plays the current playlist in the chosen order, similar to programs like

Spotify. djay automatically creates surprisingly good transitions between the tracks. This function is not only useful for taking a short break during a DJ set but also allows you to create complete DJ sets with minimal effort.

djay Pricing

- Monthly Subscription: $6.99 per month
- Annual Subscription: $49.99 per year

There is also a free version of the app, which offers only basic features. For the full range of functions, including advanced features like Neural Mix, a subscription is required. The subscription provides access to all features of the software across various platforms, including macOS, iPad, and iPhone.

Enjoy exploring djay and the fantastic possibilities it offers for modern DJing!

DJ.Studio—The DAW for DJs

Most DJ programs are designed for live performance, but often you might want to pre-produce a DJ set—for example, for a radio show. Until now, Ableton Live was the preferred program because it offers excellent features for adjusting tempo and pitch. However, Ableton Live focuses more on live music production. DJ.Studio, on the other hand, has recognized this niche and offers specially optimized software for the pre-production of DJ sets (Figure 9.1).

The program offers a variety of advanced features that enable music producers to craft their tracks more efficiently and creatively. These include

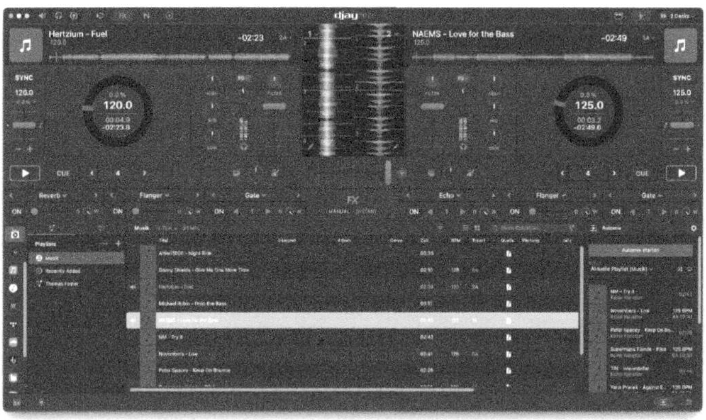

Figure 9.1 DJ.Studio's Interface for Pre-producing DJ Sets.

AI-supported features like Beatgrids, Stem Separation, Phrase Detection, Vocal Changing, and automatic track shortening. These AI tools help automate repetitive tasks, allowing you to focus on the creative aspects of music production.

You can import songs from your hard drive or insert entire playlists from Spotify or YouTube. Since direct downloads from Spotify are not possible, DJ.Studio verifies the songs via YouTube and downloads them from there. After importing, the software analyzes the tempo, key, and other properties of the tracks.

With the Automix function, DJ.Studio automatically creates a complete mix by trying out various combinations and song sequences to find the best one. All transitions can be edited and optimized afterward. Numerous transition options are available, from the typical bass swap to more creative effects like echo or scratch.

It's easy to shorten, extend, or loop songs. Additionally, you can add jingles or voice recordings on extra tracks. The finished DJ set can be exported as an audio or video file—for example, to upload it to YouTube. Exporting to Ableton Live is also possible to further edit the mix there.

For everyone who wants to pre-produce their mixes, DJ.Studio is the ideal software.

Quick Start: Creating and Exporting a DJ Set

To create a new DJ set, click on Create New Mix. Then choose whether you want to import tracks from your hard drive, Beatport, Beat Source, or YouTube. In this example, I choose tracks from my hard drive. In the next window, click on Import Local Files and select the desired WAV or MP3 files. DJ.Studio takes some time to analyze the tracks. Afterward, a window titled Automation Playlist appears, where you can make various settings regarding the order and transitions. Then click on Auto Mix to create your set, which may take a few seconds. Confirm with Finish, and your DJ set is ready. You can now listen to all transitions and optimize them if necessary.

Both at the top right of the interface and in the File menu, there is the Export function. Here you can specify whether you want to export your DJ set as an MP3 file (ideal for sharing), as a WAV file (for better audio quality), as a video (for uploading to platforms like YouTube), as a DJ set for rekordbox, or as an Ableton Live set.

All volume levels, filter automations, and the exact arrangement of the tracks are exported and made available in Ableton Live so that you can further edit your DJ set there. This integration makes DJ.Studio particularly flexible and opens up additional creative possibilities for DJs in post-production. By transferring the mixes created in DJ.Studio to a professional DAW like Ableton Live, you can make fine adjustments and perfect the mix according to your preferences.

DJ.Studio Offers Three Versions

- Studio: €99
- Pro: €149
- Pro + Stems: €199

See DJ Studio in Action

https://youtu.be/nyo6nUVfevk?si=O25de1O3ynbMRUvB&t=669

10 Generating Music Videos with AI

A New Era of Creative Production

At the end of 2022, an AI-generated video caused a stir on the internet, showing Will Smith eating spaghetti in a humorous and surrealistic way. This video spread quickly and fascinated viewers worldwide: it demonstrated that artificial intelligence is capable of creating vivid, albeit not always realistic, video scenes based on text descriptions. The scene, in which a distorted, almost caricature-like Will Smith eats spaghetti, was far from realistic, but it showcased the creative potential that AI-based technologies could offer for the future.

Just two years later, we find ourselves in an entirely new phase of AI video generation. New tools and platforms seem to emerge daily, enabling users to create impressive videos with the help of AI. This rapid development has the potential to fundamentally change the way we produce music videos by providing artists and producers with new, affordable tools to transform their creative visions into visual experiences.

However, these advances also bring challenges, particularly in areas like news and media reporting. The ability to create deceptively real videos using AI has the potential to significantly facilitate the spread of misinformation and fake news. What is a fascinating new tool for creative design for musicians and artists poses a serious problem in the realm of information dissemination. The possibility of manipulating videos in this way means that society must remain vigilant to distinguish truth from deception.

To address this challenge, there might be mandatory labeling requirements for AI-generated content on platforms like YouTube or TikTok in the future. These labels would help users recognize at first glance whether they are dealing with real or artificially generated material. Additionally, technologies could be developed that function like a "spam filter" for AI content, allowing individuals to decide for themselves whether they want to be confronted with potential misinformation. Such filtering systems could also be employed in telephone communication to detect and prevent fraudulent calls, like the so-called "grandparent scam." These approaches would help curb the misuse of AI technologies while promoting their positive creative use.

In this chapter, I want to give you an overview of the most exciting and advanced tools currently available and show how they can help musicians and

DOI: 10.4324/9781003621126-10

creatives realize their visions. Let's dive into the world of AI-assisted video production and discover how these technologies offer both challenges and opportunities for the future. Enjoy exploring!

Kling AI

A Leading AI Tool for Video Generation

Kling AI is one of the most advanced AI tools currently available for creating videos based on text descriptions. Developed by Kuaishou, a Chinese technology company, Kling AI enables users worldwide to produce high-quality videos with just a few inputs. Originally, the use of Kling AI was restricted to Chinese users due to registration requirements; it required a Chinese phone number or the use of the Kwai Cut app, which is only available in Chinese. But that has changed: recently, anyone worldwide can register using a simple email address to utilize the AI.

With Kling AI, users can not only generate impressive images but also create videos in two different lengths: 5 or 10 seconds. There are two options for video creation: either start with a text prompt that describes in detail what should be seen in the video or use an image as a starting point to generate a dynamic video based on it. The simple user interface and versatile options make Kling AI a particularly creative tool for artists, filmmakers, and content creators.

Starting from the international version 1.0, users have 66 free credits available daily, enough for about six short image-to-video clips. Additional credits can be purchased if needed. The platform supports various features, including the ability to roughly determine the camera movement in the video, and more features are planned, such as an editing function to further refine videos after generation.

While international users currently enjoy the basic version of Kling AI, the Chinese version already offers advanced features like video extensions (to lengthen existing videos), end frames, removing the watermark, and an HQ mode. Additionally, 10-second videos can already be generated in the Chinese version, which has not yet been unlocked in international markets.

However, Kling AI faces the challenge of keeping up with high demand. Currently, generating a video can take several hours or may get stuck at 99%. It is expected that Kuaishou will soon allocate more resources to resolve this issue.

My friend and YouTube colleague Lee Esposito showed me some of his impressive results generated with Kling AI. In one of his tests, he used the same text prompt that was used in Sora's famous example—the scene of an Asian woman walking through a busy Asian street at night.

"A stylish woman walks down a Tokyo street filled with warm glowing neon and animated city signage. She wears a black leather jacket, a long red dress, and black boots, and carries a black purse. She wears sunglasses and red lipstick. She walks confidently and casually. The street is damp and reflective, creating a mirror effect of the colorful lights. Many pedestrians walk about."

The prompt describes a scene where a stylish woman walks down a busy street in Tokyo, illuminated by warm glowing neon lights and animated city signs. She wears a black leather jacket, a long red dress, black boots, and carries a black purse. She also wears sunglasses and red lipstick. The street is damp and reflective, creating a mirror effect of the colorful lights, while many pedestrians pass by.

Kling AI's result was also impressive, especially due to the lifelike reflections on the wet ground and the convincing depictions of the other pedestrians. However, the woman's face did not reach the level of detail and quality that we know from Sora, indicating that Kling AI is not yet quite on par in certain areas.

Another example that Lee created was a scene where two pirate ships are battling inside a coffee cup. This video really blew me away because it was visually extremely convincing and creatively executed. The combination of fantastic imagination and technical implementation showcases Kling AI's potential to generate unique and fascinating videos.

However, the results were less impressive when converting still images to videos. Lee reported that his tests in this area almost consistently failed. Even though the rendering times were pleasantly short—averaging only 2–5 minutes—the results often fell short of expectations. It became apparent that simpler prompts led to better results, suggesting that the technology still needs optimization in this area.

My Experiment with Kling AI

In my own experiment with Kling AI's text-to-video function, I used the prompt: "A man and a dog are walking on the keys of a synthesizer." The rendering time was about 40 minutes before it stalled at 99%. After waiting another hour, I decided to let the process run overnight. The next morning, the video was finally complete.

Unfortunately, the result did not quite match my vision of a small man and a dog strolling over the large keys of a synthesizer. Instead, the video showed a man sitting with his dog at a synthesizer. But what fascinated me was how real and convincing both the man and the synthesizer appeared. There were no discernible signs that the video was created using artificial intelligence—at least not in the depiction of the man and the dog.

However, there were two clues indicating that it was an AI-generated video. First, as someone who knows almost all synthesizer models, I immediately noticed that this synthesizer does not exist in reality. Most striking, however, was the depiction of the keyboard's keys: instead of the usual pattern of three black keys, followed by two, and then three black keys again, this synthesizer keyboard showed a faulty sequence—first three, then four, then two, and finally even six black keys. Such deviations are a known problem with many AI tools and show that despite the impressive visual quality, there are still challenges in achieving detail accuracy.

Luma Dream Machine

A Breakthrough in AI-Assisted Video Generation

Released on June 12, 2024, the Dream Machine by Luma Labs, a San Francisco-based AI startup, is among the leading tools for creating videos based on text prompts. This AI-powered video generation platform is built on a scalable and efficient transformer architecture trained directly on videos. This allows it to produce physically consistent and realistic scenes characterized by high quality and detail.

The Dream Machine enables users to create videos up to five seconds long with a resolution of 1360 × 752 pixels by either entering a text prompt or using a static image as a starting point. The tool can also integrate smooth and cinematic camera movements, selectable through a simple menu. Movement options include "Move Left," "Pan Right," or "Zoom In," among others. These features offer unprecedented control over the final result and open up a wide range of creative possibilities.

Since the introduction of the Dream Machine, Luma Labs has continuously added new features, including the ability to extend videos, edit them, and remove watermarks. The latest version 1.6 provides even more control over camera movements and allows users to precisely define the desired camera perspectives. With these enhancements, Luma Labs aims to compete with other leading AI video tools like OpenAI's Sora and Kuaishou's Kling AI.

The first text prompt I tried was: "A dolphin swims in a soup that's on the table." The result was impressive: the soup and the table were rendered extremely realistically and immediately convinced me. The dolphin itself also looked very convincing in the first few seconds. However, the depiction became increasingly less convincing as the dolphin moved and seemed to hover above the soup rather than actually swimming in it. This shows that despite its remarkable capabilities, the Dream Machine still has room for improvement, especially when it comes to more complex motion representations.

Interestingly, my friend Lee experienced that the Dream Machine delivers particularly good results when it comes to turning an image into a video. He achieved his best results with this type of application, indicating that the Dream Machine is particularly mature in this area.

The platform currently offers various subscription levels—from Standard to Premier—that allow users a certain number of videos per month. Dream Machine was developed to simplify creative processes and give users the ability to generate realistic and high-quality videos in an intuitive way.

Neural Frames

A Unique AI Tool for Artistic Music Videos

Neural Frames immediately caught my interest because, unlike many other AI tools, it doesn't come from Asia or America but from Germany. This tool offers a unique approach to video generation: it allows users to create or upload images, which are then transformed into fluid animations using AI. Neural Frames utilizes advanced AI models like Stable Diffusion, known for converting text descriptions into fluid motion animations while achieving impressive quality.

In my initial experiments, I uploaded very realistic images of people and landscapes to transform them into animations. However, the results didn't convince me; the representations often appeared stiff and somewhat unnatural. But I noticed that Neural Frames has a special talent for generating animations from certain graphic elements and abstract motifs that resemble modern art and are excellent for creative music videos.

The more I began to use surreal and abstract motifs like spaceships, geometric patterns, or artistic designs, the more convincing the results became. These experimental animations exuded a unique visual aesthetic that perfectly fits modern music videos. Neural Frames' potential to develop new visual styles creatively sets it apart from other AI tools and makes it an ideal tool for musicians and artists looking for something extraordinary.

A good example is my song "Echoes," for which I used Neural Frames to create surreal, dreamlike visuals that perfectly complement the song's atmosphere. The ability of Neural Frames to create something new and fascinating from seemingly ordinary graphics is impressive and has led me to use it regularly for my music videos.

The strength of Neural Frames lies in its flexibility and the ability to influence the final result by adjusting text prompts or uploading new images. Especially in combination with surrealistic or abstract art styles, this tool shows its full potential. It is a great example of how artificial intelligence can be used in the creative production of music videos to create original and captivating visual experiences.

Krea.ai

An Innovative AI Tool for Creative Video Production

Krea.ai offers a versatile platform that enables users to generate content in creative and innovative ways. On Krea.ai's homepage, you'll find several tools, each offering different functions and creative possibilities. One of the standout features is the ability to upscale images and videos to high resolutions, which is particularly appreciated in the world of digital art and content creation.

However, the most exciting tool from Krea.ai is its video generation function. Instead of relying on traditional text-to-video algorithms, Krea.ai provides a timeline-based interface where users can place various images. The AI then creatively connects and animates these images into a cohesive video. This process allows for complex and artistic transitions between individual images, which are often surprising and innovative.

An impressive example of applying this technology comes from my friend and YouTube colleague Lee Esposito, who conceptualized a complete music video. Lee generated a new image for each scene of his storyboard, each lasting 10 seconds, and then had Krea.ai's AI artfully connect these images. The end result is a visually captivating music video that isn't necessarily realistic but stands out through seamless transitions and creative morphing between the images. This technique opens up entirely new possibilities for visual storytelling in music videos and creates an immersive experience for the viewer.

YouTube Video: AI MUSIC VIDEO | MIDNIGHT WHISPERS by LOVE+GRAVITY

https://youtu.be/1hMniUBllfQ

Another particularly impressive aspect is the ability to influence the generated images live on Krea.ai. Lee demonstrated in another example how he implements creative inputs in real-time using simple means like a webcam. In an impressive YouTube video, he shows how he holds a rope in his hand with a simple webcam, which the AI later transforms into a snake in the generated video, or how he pets a pillow, which then becomes a sheep in the video.

YouTube Video: KREA AI TEST | LIVE AI CAMERA

https://youtu.be/SkR3RX3J5TI

This technique allows users to directly incorporate their creative ideas into the video by drawing, shaping, or using live camera feeds, providing a truly dynamic and interactive experience.

In summary, Krea.ai is a remarkable tool for video creation, suitable for both beginners and professional creatives. It offers a simple and intuitive user interface along with powerful features that enable artists to create imaginative and impressive content.

LTX Studio

A Versatile AI Tool for Creative Video Concepts and Prototypes

LTX Studio, developed by Lightricks—a company founded in Jerusalem in 2013 and known for its popular photo and video editing apps like Facetune—offers an innovative platform for creating and editing videos using artificial intelligence. In 2024, Lightricks launched LTX Studio, a tool that enables users to present their visions for videos in a visually compelling way.

LTX Studio is particularly useful for creative professionals who want to make their concepts visible to clients. The tool allows you to insert characters and storyboards, which are then transformed into convincingly realistic images and animations. While the movements in the generated videos aren't perfect yet—tending more toward still images with slight movements and camera pans—the potential is clearly there. With the right story and a well-thought-out approach, you could not only create concept prototypes but also genuinely exciting and engaging videos for creative projects.

A significant advantage of LTX Studio is the flexibility it offers users after the video has been generated. It's possible to edit and define individual characters—for example, changing their clothing or appearance—even after the entire video is completed. These adjustments are easy to carry out thanks to the intuitive user interface and powerful AI-driven editing tools. You can also edit individual scenes in the video by selecting specific areas in the images and using a prompt to describe how they should be changed.

The adaptability of LTX Studio allows you to refine the video and tailor it precisely to the requirements of a project. For creative professionals who want to capture their ideas in visually impressive storyboards and prototypes, LTX Studio offers a powerful and flexible tool.

HEDRA

A Creative Solution for Synchronizing Vocals with AI

When Netflix released the fourth installment of Beverly Hills Cop, I had the idea, together with a friend who used to work with Harold Faltermeyer—the composer of the iconic synthesizer riff "Axel F."—to create a reinterpretation of this famous song. Our concept was to combine the well-known synthesizer motif with vocals and have it performed by a female singer. We were all amazed at how well it worked to have this distinctive synthesizer melody sung by a human voice. However, for the accompanying music video, we had a specific visual in mind: we wanted to see a policewoman singing this melody.

After some research, I came across the platform HEDRA, which turned out to be just the right tool for our project. HEDRA is an AI-powered video tool that allows users to create animated videos where uploaded characters or images can be synchronized in real-time with uploaded audio. It offers an intuitive and user-friendly interface that's easy to operate even without prior knowledge in video editing.

We used HEDRA by uploading a photo of a policewoman that I had previously created using the AI platform Midjourney. Additionally, we uploaded the a cappella version of the vocals. Within minutes, we received a finished video in which the policewoman from the image sang the chorus of our remake in sync. The simplicity of the process and the quality of the result were impressive and fulfilled exactly what we had envisioned.

Why HEDRA Is a Unique Tool

HEDRA stands out due to its focus on ease of use and accessibility. It's free to use, making it appealing to creatives who want to implement their ideas quickly without significant expenses. A particularly helpful tip when using HEDRA is to upload the vocals without reverb or other effects and without playback—in other words, preferably just the dry vocal track. This makes it easier for the AI to synchronize and leads to a more natural result.

The goal of HEDRA is to give everyone the opportunity to realize their own creative vision, whether through the creation of new worlds, characters, or stories.

YouTube Video: Axel F—Thomas Foster Techno Cop • Beverly Hills Cop

LivePortrait

An Innovative Tool for Animating Images Through Videos

LivePortrait is a creative AI tool that allows static images to come to life by using control videos to make them speak or sing. Unlike other tools like HEDRA, which use audio, LivePortrait relies on video recordings as a control source. Users can upload a video of themselves speaking, singing, or displaying facial expressions, and then choose an image that mimics these movements and expressions. The result is an animated version of the image that precisely follows the movements and expressions in the control video.

This tool is particularly useful for creative projects where lifelike animations of characters, historical figures, or artistic portraits are desired. Users can create innovative videos by transforming simple photos into vivid, expressive animations.

Developed by a research team from the Chinese Kuaishou Corporation—also responsible for the well-known video AI tool Kling—LivePortrait offers new possibilities for interactive and creative animation of images and videos. By releasing the inference code and models as an open-source project on GitHub, developers and users can freely use and adapt the algorithm.

LivePortrait is a powerful tool for filmmakers, artists, and creatives who want to create realistic and expressive animations with minimal effort. It provides a new form of visual representation that brings traditional static images to life, thereby expanding storytelling possibilities.

Conclusion: The Future of Music Video Generation with Artificial Intelligence

After extensive testing of the leading tools for generating music videos with artificial intelligence, I've come to an important realization: these technologies are still in development and far from perfect. The error rate is high, and many of the created videos still have qualitative deficiencies. Generating a video can take a long time—often hours—and the end result rarely matches the quality of professional video production expected from traditional methods.

Despite these challenges, it's fascinating to see how far the technology has already come. The ability to animate complex visual scenarios, movements, and even singing opens up completely new avenues for creatives to realize their ideas. What's exciting about these tools is that they already offer significant potential for artistic expression, creating new opportunities for musicians, video artists, and filmmakers who want to stand out with limited resources.

I'm convinced that it's only a matter of a few years before these tools reach a high level of perfection. The continuous development of the algorithms and models used in these AI systems will minimize errors and significantly improve the quality of the generated content. But there's also a downside: once these technologies are fully mature and widespread, they will no longer be anything special. The innovative character and creative potential they offer today could then be lost.

Therefore, we're currently in an exciting transitional phase. The technology isn't mature yet, but it allows us to create something truly unique with minimal effort and a lot of creativity. This is the moment when these tools can be seen not just as aids but as new forms of expression. For creatives willing to embrace the new, now is the ideal time to engage with these technologies and use them to create something unique that stands out from the crowd.

In the end, it's about how we use these tools to expand and enrich our artistic vision. The art lies not only in the technology itself but in how we apply it to create new and unforgettable experiences. In a time when technology is rapidly evolving, those who are willing to engage early with these new tools have the chance to set the creative standard of tomorrow.

SORA—Text-to-Video by OpenAI

OpenAI first introduced its text-to-video model, SORA, on February 15, 2024. At the time, they amazed us with video footage that looked incredibly realistic, significantly surpassing anything available up to that point. The most famous examples are probably the Saint Bernard puppies playing in the snow, or the stylish woman strolling through the streets of Tokyo.

The possibilities offered by SORA are revolutionary and open entirely new avenues in video production. What once required a large team of up to 20 people—including directors, camera operators, lighting technicians, and assistants—can now be replaced by a simple text prompt. Street closures, camera dollies, elaborate lighting setups, and catering trucks are a thing of the past. Previously, such a shoot would have required several days of preparation and at least €20,000 to €50,000. In contrast, with SORA, videos of similarly high quality can be created within seconds—at no additional cost. This not only makes the technology highly attractive to creatives and media professionals, but also turns the entire industry on its head.

The official release of SORA took place on December 9, 2024. At that time, however, only ChatGPT Plus and Pro subscribers in the U.S. and some other countries had access to it.

User Interface and Features

Once logged in, the left side of the interface displays several well-structured menus to facilitate navigation and content organization:

1 Explore

- Recent: Shows the latest videos created by other users.
- Featured: Contains videos selected by OpenAI that demonstrate exceptional quality or creativity.
- Saved: Stores all videos where the user clicked the "Save" button, similar to bookmarks.

2 Library

- All Videos: Displays all videos you have generated yourself.
- Favorites: Lists the videos you have marked as favorites.
- Uploads: A collection of files you have uploaded to the platform for further processing.

3 Organizational Tools

- New Folder: Allows you to create new folders to better organize your work.
- Additional folders created by the user, such as "Physics" or "MKBHD," can also be managed here.

Learning by Observation

A particularly interesting feature of SORA is the ability to view the text prompts used for each video. For every video in "Recent" or "Featured," the prompt that generated it is displayed. This makes it possible to understand how simple or detailed these prompts can be and how they influence the final result. It's a fantastic learning opportunity to improve your own prompts and achieve the best possible outcomes.

Remix Feature: Adjusting Existing Videos

One of SORA's standout features is the Remix button available under each video. When you click this button, a menu appears where you can request specific changes to the video. This menu allows the following adjustments:

1 Version: Choose the desired version of the remix.
2 Resolution: Set the video quality, such as 1080p.

3 Remix Intensity: Several options are available here:

- Strong: Significant changes to the original video
- Mild: Noticeable but moderate changes
- Subtle: Slight adjustments that barely alter the original
- Custom: Allows for individualized customization of the remix intensity

Once you've made your selections, you click Remix and receive the edited video shortly thereafter.

Example: A Drone Flight with the Remix Feature

An impressive example presented by Marques Brownlee demonstrates the power of this function. In his video, a drone flew over a house on a hill. For the remixed version, he specified that he wanted to see a golf course behind the house. The result was astonishing: instead of the original lawn, the remixed video showed the same drone flight, but with a perfectly integrated golf course behind the house. This example highlights just how realistic and flexible editing with SORA can be.

The Storyboard Feature

Creating Scenes with a Cohesive Look

A truly impressive feature of SORA is the Storyboard tool. Right in the text field where you enter your prompt for a video, you'll find a Storyboard button. Once clicked, you can create multiple shorter prompts, each of which generates its own short scene.

What's special about the Storyboard feature is that it's ideal for producing multiple scenes with a cohesive look and consistent style. As a result, the scenes don't feel like random clips pieced together, but rather form a harmonious whole. This tool is particularly interesting for users who want to create longer videos or stories composed of multiple scenes that are visually and thematically aligned.

Uploads: "Bringing Photos to Life"

Under the Uploads section, you can upload photos and then use a text prompt to instruct SORA on how to extend that photo into a video. This feature opens up exciting possibilities for personal projects. Who wouldn't be thrilled to upload an old baby photo from their childhood and have it transformed into a moving scene? Or take a photo of you and your teenage sweetheart and use SORA to create a story that perhaps never actually happened? These scenarios not only bring creative visions to life but also evoke nostalgic memories in a completely new, interactive way.

On SORA's Quality: "Impressive, But Not Perfect"

SORA's quality is sometimes extremely impressive, making it very hard—or almost impossible—to distinguish its output from real footage. Particularly scenes with realistic lighting and shadow effects, complex camera movements, and vivid colors can easily pass as professionally filmed videos.

However, on closer inspection, SORA is not yet perfect. Errors often occur that reveal the model's AI origins. For example, objects people hold in their hands might suddenly disappear or appear out of nowhere. Additionally, when humans or animals move, their movements can sometimes look off—legs might be positioned incorrectly, or motions appear unnatural. Such inconsistencies make it relatively easy, especially for trained eyes, to spot that these are AI-generated videos.

Still, it's remarkable how quickly this technology is evolving. Errors that stand out today might be fixed by tomorrow's updates. Considering how rapidly other AI tools have advanced in recent months, it's reasonable to expect that SORA will soon make far fewer mistakes. It's entirely possible that the videos will become so realistic that even experts will struggle to distinguish them from genuine footage.

A Thank You

Special thanks go to my friend and YouTube colleague Lee Esposito from the channel Alphatester for his support in researching the tools for this chapter. He not only provided valuable suggestions but also carefully reviewed the text to ensure everything is coherent and correct.

11 The Soundmakers of the Future

A Journey through the History and Future of AI in Music

Let me take you on a journey through the history of music and artificial intelligence. Our journey begins in the past, where early pioneers laid the foundations for computer-generated music, and simultaneously casts a glance into the future to discover what awaits us in the coming years.

Already in 1957, the two Americans Lejaren Hiller and Leonard Isaacson programmed the ILLIAC computer, which created the first work entirely composed by a computer: the "ILLIAC Suite." This string quartet utilized a combination of random generators, rhythmic and dynamic variations, and the twelve-tone technique to emulate musical rules and structures. The "ILLIAC Suite" is considered an early example of algorithmic composition, where not just random tones were generated but complex musical principles were applied by the computer. This method laid the groundwork for the further development of computer-generated music and demonstrated that computers are capable of creating music that follows traditional compositional rules.

In 1987, David Cope developed the computer program EMI, short for "Experiments in Musical Intelligence." This program was a groundbreaking step in computer-assisted composition, as it was capable of generating works in the style of Bach, Mozart, Beethoven, and other classical composers, which sounded so authentic that even experts often had difficulty distinguishing them from the originals. EMI analyzed the works of famous composers and identified their unique musical patterns to create new compositions. This ability to imitate human compositional styles and create new works was a milestone in AI-supported music production and sparked a profound debate about whether machines are capable of genuine creativity or merely mimic existing styles.

In 1995, David Bowie, together with his programmer friend Ty Roberts, developed the software Verbasizer, an innovative text-generation tool considered an early example of computer-assisted creativity. With Verbasizer, Bowie could create song lyrics by combining and rearranging various text fragments from newspaper articles and other sources. Bowie described the result as "a real kaleidoscope of meanings, themes, nouns, and verbs that all collide in some way." This technique allowed him to craft creative, unpredictable lyrical structures that stood out from traditional writing processes.

DOI: 10.4324/9781003621126-11

Roberts programmed the software for the Mac, and Bowie used this method to inspire the writing process for his albums Outside, Earthling, and Hours.... Verbasizer served Bowie as a tool to break through his creative routine and explore new artistic paths that contributed to his unique music.

In 2015, Google launched Project Magenta, an open-source initiative exploring the possibilities of machine learning in creative music production. Magenta utilized advanced neural networks to generate music and art and served as a platform for artists and researchers who wanted to explore the potential of AI in creative processes. Under the name Magenta Studio, Google released a series of "Max for Live" tools that could be seamlessly integrated into the music production software Ableton Live. These tools allowed musicians to generate new melodies or combine two existing, user-created MIDI clips to create a new composition. Magenta Studio enabled musicians and producers to experiment with AI-powered functions, significantly expanding their creative possibilities. The project contributed significantly to popularizing the use of AI in music production and inspired numerous further innovations in AI-generated art.

A year later, in 2018, Taryn Southern released the first album entirely composed with artificial intelligence. She used a program called Amper Music and named the album I AM AI.

By 2021, most AI projects focused on generating music and lyrics without covering the entire production process. The major turning point came in 2021 when OpenAI, a company originally co-founded by Elon Musk, released the project Jukebox. This advanced neural network went beyond previous approaches by not only generating notes and lyrics but also producing complete, audible songs as audio files. For the first time in history, we could hear music that was entirely composed, written, arranged, and mixed by artificial intelligence—including the simulation of all instruments and vocals. While Jukebox represented a significant technological breakthrough, the quality of the generated audio files suffered from heavy compression, which often made the music sound like a poorly encoded MP3. This compression was necessary to reduce the enormous data volumes of the millions of analyzed songs. Despite this limitation, Jukebox marked a decisive step toward a future where AI could produce music that is hardly distinguishable from that produced by humans. It became clear that the ability of computers to create realistic music productions is only a matter of time and technological advancement.

In the following years, more projects appeared, such as Google's MusicLM, Adobe's Project Music GenA, and several others. With each new project, the quality of the music and audio files improved. In December 2023, the time had come: the projects Suno and Udio gave their users the ability to generate music on their respective websites within seconds—music that I claim is very hard to distinguish from that produced by humans. Since December 2023, it should be clear to everyone: in the future, machines will create music.

References

Bowie, D. (1995). Interview with Ty Roberts about the development of Verbasizer. Rolling Stone Magazine. Retrieved from https://www.rollingstone.com

Cope, D. (1987). Experiments in Musical Intelligence (EMI). *Computer Music Journal*, 11(4), 19–35. DOI: 10.2307/3677234

Google Magenta. (2016). Project Magenta. Retrieved from https://magenta.tensorflow.org/

Hiller, L., & Isaacson, L. (1957). The "Illiac" Suite for String Quartet. *Computer Music Journal*, 1(4), 15–32. DOI: 10.2307/3677431

OpenAI. (2020). Jukebox: A Generative Model for Music. Retrieved from https://openai.com/jukebox

Southern, T. (2017). I AM AI [Album]. Retrieved from https://www.tarynsouthern.com

Suno AI. (2023). Website. Retrieved from https://suno.ai

Udio. (2023). Website. Retrieved from https://udio.com

The Present and Future of AI in Music

Now one might ask the question: Are we already listening to music today that was generated by artificial intelligence without knowing it? What percentage of music on Spotify is already made by AI? There are no official figures on this, but I can say the following: I know some producers who have found a way to publish music on Spotify and generate an income sufficient to support their families. In this kind of music, it's not so much about quality but much more about quantity. A good friend of mine uploads a new album with chill-out music every week, and an acquaintance claims to make a living by releasing over 1,000 electronic music songs every month. The Spotify algorithm rewards this high frequency of uploads, and while these are not big hits, the sheer volume brings success. These two friends of mine are certainly not isolated cases. I have already seen several YouTube tutorials that explain step by step how to generate music with AI, upload it to Spotify, and make money from it. If Amazon is preventing users from uploading more than 30 books per day that are completely written by AI, then we can assume that many users are making a living by uploading works they have generated with Suno or Udio.

And even though we can assume that the quality of systems like Suno and Udio will continue to increase in the coming years, I do not believe that the big hits of the world will be generated exclusively by AI in the future. It is likely that soon 10% or more of the songs on Spotify could be produced by AI. Nevertheless, I am convinced that new hits by artists like Taylor Swift or David Guetta will still be created by human hands even in ten years—possibly with the support of AI technology. Why? There are several reasons for this. First, record labels continue to invest significant sums in the production of hits: music videos, marketing campaigns like radio promotion, press releases, DJ sampling, and placement in important Spotify playlists are expensive. Such investments will only be made by labels in music that they consider truly promising and are convinced of its success. Second, consumers demand performers they can follow on social networks to gain insights into their creative processes and personal stories. In a world where authenticity and the human element are still highly valued, the artist as a person will continue to play a central role—even if AI stands by as a creative partner.

Three interesting paths emerge as to how artificial intelligence could influence our music in the coming years. First, the knowledge embedded in AI programs like Suno and Udio could be integrated into our music production programs (DAWs) in the form of many individual functions and support us in producing. Second, AI could help us to better create electronic live music. And third, I see AI-generated music that is produced at the moment we hear it—live, under the motto "The soundtrack to your life." I would like to delve into all three paths:

AI in the DAW

When we look at Suno and Udio, AI programs that are capable of creating a complete song based on a text prompt, many abilities are combined: composing, writing lyrics, arranging, mixing, mastering, as well as generating vocals and instruments. If all these functions were integrated as individual functions into our DAWs like Logic Pro, Ableton Live, FL Studio, Cubase, etc., the following functions could emerge:

Composing

The DAW could support us in composing by making harmony suggestions, writing melodies over a chord progression, and taking into account factors such as the music style, an existing text, and already present vocals or melodies.

Lyric Writing

Since the use of ChatGPT, many of us already use AI for lyric writing. This could be further optimized by enabling the AI to write lyrics to an existing melody.

Arranging

Some music programs, like Logic Pro, have introduced the so-called chord track, where the chords of the song are found and to which other tracks can react. I see no reason why in the future complete arrangements should not react to such chord tracks. Instead of inserting notes on each track or playing them via a keyboard, there could be an AI assistant on each track that responds to the basic composition appropriate to the respective music style.

Mixing

One of the most important processes for a good-sounding music production is mixing. Here, the volume, panorama, sound, and various effects like reverb, delay, distortion, etc., are set for each track or instrument. Although there are already various software approaches that promise to support us in mixing, most have not convinced me so far. But I am sure that will change.

Mastering

In the past, finished mixed productions were sent to a mastering studio, where the stereo file was once again checked and adjusted for sound and dynamics. Some still use these external mastering studios today, but many producers, like me, choose to do the mastering in the stereo sum of the DAW. This brings many advantages because you already hear the final sound while mixing and do not have to send the project back to the mastering studio when changes are made in the mix. Here, too, there are already initial approaches like the Mastering Assistant from Logic Pro or the website Landr, where you can upload the track online to receive the version mastered by AI. Nevertheless, much still needs to happen here to have the quality of a piece mastered by humans matched by the machine.

Vocals

The generation of vocals through artificial intelligence has made remarkable progress in recent years. Current tools, such as Synthesizer V, already allow for the creation of artificial voices to be integrated into music productions. However, these technologies are still at the beginning of their possibilities and are often quite limited in terms of voice variety and language support.

Imagine a tool fully integrated into your DAW that allows you to generate vocals from scratch—as easily and flexibly as using a synthesizer. This tool would allow you to compose a melody and then select a choir to sing this melody. You would have the choice between different types of choirs such as a children's choir, a gospel choir, a women's choir, a jazz choir, or a classical choir.

Then, of course, it would make sense to generate multi-part choirs. You could, for example, create an 80-piece classical choir consisting of soprano, alto, tenor, and bass voices, singing in perfect harmony and with the precision and richness of sound of a real performance. The voices could be individually adjusted—from pitch to timbre to the type of articulation—to achieve the desired emotional expression. All this could happen in a seamless workflow within the DAW without the use of external tools or extensive recording sessions.

Additionally, it would be crucial that this tool offers broad support for different languages. While current solutions are often limited to English, Japanese, and Chinese, this future technology would enable the creation of choirs in all common languages, including Spanish, Italian, German, French, and many more. This expansion would not only broaden the creative scope but also facilitate access to new markets and target groups by making music production more international and diverse.

Instruments

Music programs can already generate instruments or sounds today. Essentially, there are two techniques: the synthesizer and the sampler. When it comes to imitating real instruments, sampling is mostly used. Here, individual tones of the respective instrument are recorded in different pitches, dynamic levels, and playing techniques. These recordings can later be played like an instrument via a keyboard. Companies like the Vienna Symphonic Library sell their own libraries for individual instruments or instrument groups. Such libraries can be several hundred gigabytes in size. These instruments could be generated by AI in the future. This could lead to such a library being only a few megabytes in size and sounding more convincing than previous sampling.

Live Performing with AI

When we watch a DJ at work today, his task, besides selecting the songs, essentially consists of mixing them. Although DJ programs offer more and more features to mix beats, loops, and samples live, this unfortunately happens only rarely in practice. Most DJs give the impression of creating the dynamics of the songs live on the DJ mixer, which in many cases unfortunately does not correspond to reality. With this statement, I do not intend to belittle the work of these DJs; DJs deserve my utmost admiration. Nevertheless, successful entertainment is an equally important component of this job.

Ultimately, a good club track often takes a day or even several days to work on, and it is almost impossible to deliver everything spontaneously in a live performance. Some musicians do make an effort to implement such performances live; most use the program Ableton Live for this. However, this only works if a lot of time is invested in preparation to be able to quickly retrieve the sounds in the live performance.

However, this could change significantly with AI. AI could be a kind of musician and sound assistant in a live performance, supporting us in generating club music and other music styles live in a quality that is hard to distinguish from a track elaborately produced in the studio.

The Soundtrack of Your Life

If the computing power of our computers, smartphones, etc., continues to develop as it has in recent years, AI will soon be able to generate music in real-time, i.e., at the moment we hear it. Instead of listening to a recording of music made in the past, the music could be generated for this situation at this moment. It could take into account various factors to fit better into the respective situation than music played from a canned source.

Voices

Vocals can be very distracting when they compete with conversations. If you are having a conversation and music with vocals is playing in the background, these vocals can overlay and distract from the conversation. Therefore, an AI could analyze whether people are currently talking and in such moments reduce or completely omit the vocals in the music to create a more pleasant background atmosphere.

Tonality of the Environment

Many sounds in our environment have a certain mood or pitch. These sounds can compete with the music or sound dissonant. An AI could adjust the tonality of the music and omit noise frequencies to achieve a harmonious effect.

Rhythm of the Environment

Often, environmental noises create a rhythm that does not match the music. An AI could adjust this rhythm to create better harmony between the environment and the music.

Walking or Running Pace

The tempo of our movement when walking or jogging could differ from that of the music and be perceived as disturbing. AI-generated music could adapt to our walking pace.

Biometric Data

By capturing biometric data such as heart rate, breathing rate, or skin conductivity, the music could react to our emotional and physical state and adjust its dynamics.

Artificial Intelligence and the Revival of the Depeche Mode Sound

Recently, I discovered a song on YouTube titled "Artificial Intelligence Depeche Mode's song, originally created and uploaded from @andrea_fryer," which was generated in the style of Depeche Mode and originally uploaded by Andrea Fryer. I was astonished at how much this song actually sounds like a real Depeche Mode song—so much so that I would have been completely fooled if someone had told me it was a new track by the band. The music captures the essence of the iconic Depeche Mode style, with the deep, dark synth melodies and the typical mood characteristic of the band.

This discovery piqued my curiosity, and I began to research how this song came about. It turned out that it was generated with the AI platform Udio. Fascinated by this technology, I tried it myself and entered the command: "Make a Depeche Mode song." The result was astonishing: a song that could seamlessly fit into the band's work. Although the platform states that it does not generate songs in the style of well-known artists, the result was nevertheless strongly inspired by Depeche Mode and sounded amazingly authentic.

This experience opens up a fascinating thought experiment about where the journey could go in the future. Many iconic bands no longer exist today, and their fans often miss new music from their idols. AI could be able to fill this gap by generating entire albums in the style of bands that no longer exist. But how could this technology be integrated into existing music platforms in the future?

Let's imagine how this could look on platforms like Spotify: The user clicks on a song they particularly like—for example, a classic by Depeche Mode—and not only gets the option to play similar songs from Spotify's existing database but could also have a completely new kind of playlist created. One click is enough, and the platform generates a playlist of new, never-before-heard songs that are created by an AI in real-time in the style of this song or band. These AI-generated songs could analyze the musical features, instrumentation, melody lines, and even the lyrical themes of the selected song and, based on this data, create new, unique pieces.

The idea that one receives a playlist with music that has never existed before but exactly meets the listener's taste could revolutionize the way we discover and experience music. While today's algorithms can already find and suggest similar music, this approach would go a step further: You don't just experience a variation of known songs but actually "new" music that is created in real-time and just for you.

Such playlists could be dynamic and infinitely expandable—based on the user's preferences and constantly updated with fresh, AI-generated tracks that perfectly fit the preferred style. This vision illustrates how profoundly AI could change our music landscape by giving us the ability not only to draw on past music styles but to re-experience them creatively. We could, in the future, experience the music of bands like The Beatles, Queen, or even Falco as if they had never stopped making music—all made possible through the power of artificial intelligence.

What Does the Development of AI Mean for Us Musicians?

As I mentioned at the beginning of the book, we are experiencing a change that cannot be stopped and will fundamentally alter the way we make and produce music—even more so than the introduction of the computer when we all still recorded with tape machines. This development brings challenges but also immense opportunities. For me personally, it is especially important not to ignore this trend but to be actively involved and explore the possibilities that these new technologies offer. As musicians, we should ask ourselves: Which of these new possibilities help me to produce my music faster or more effectively, and which do I integrate into my creative process?

However, I am convinced that the classic ways of music production will continue to exist. Just as there are still bands today that go into the studio and record live together—just like Frank Sinatra once did—there will continue to be room for authentic, handmade music. This way of making music creates something special, which in our technology-driven time represents a rarer and therefore more valuable experience.

One of the most profound changes that artificial intelligence brings to music, however, happens in people's minds. It is a development that began even before the spread of AI and is now becoming even more intense: Many believe that music today is simply created by computers or artificial intelligence and that music production almost works by itself. This creates the impression that behind many of today's successful music works, there is hardly any real work and that the creative process is less valuable. But it will be all the more important in the future that listeners experience an artist who is authentic and brings their passion and personality into their music.

A good example of the importance of authenticity in music history is the project Enigma, which Michael Cretu launched in the early 1990s. At that time, it was an innovative idea to keep the creator behind the music hidden. This strategy was new and fascinated the audience, leading to millions of albums sold. Today, however, I consider this approach less suitable. People want to know that the music they hear comes from a real artist. They want to experience the person behind the sounds and feel the passion and commitment with which they embody their music.

The Morning After the Big Performance

After the triumphant performance in Berlin, Sam Space returned to his hometown of Frankfurt the next morning. He woke up in his spacious loft as his personal AI, Alexa, gently roused him with the words: "Good morning, Sam. It's 8:00 AM. Your new single 'Dancing on the Rainbow' has just debuted at number one on the Billboard charts. Congratulations!"

Sam smiled sleepily and stretched in his bed. "Thank you, Alexa. Is there anything else I should know?"

"Yes, Sam," Alexa replied. "You've received 1,637 new messages. 74% of them congratulate you on yesterday's concert and praise your performance. 22% contain questions about the concert, most of which I've already answered. Additionally, there are some collaboration requests."

Sam raised an eyebrow. "Is there anyone important among them?"

"Yes," said Alexa. "Universal Pictures wants to produce a film with you."

Sam smiled with delight. "That sounds exciting. Please note that I'll address that email tomorrow at my leisure."

"Will do, Sam," Alexa confirmed.

Sam nodded and got up. "That sounds great, Alexa. Yes, please play some relaxing music."

"Will do, Sam," Alexa affirmed and began playing a gentle melody while Sam enjoyed his espresso. After getting dressed, he set off for his brunch meeting with Peter.

In a cozy café in downtown Frankfurt, Sam met his old friend Peter. Peter was thrilled about the previous night's performance and could hardly contain his admiration.

"Sam, the concert yesterday was incredible!" Peter began, biting into his croissant. "Your music sounds so different from anything out there today. How do you do it?"

Sam smiled mysteriously. "A magician never reveals his tricks."

Peter wouldn't give up. "Come on, Sam. At least give me a little insight. I'd love to see your studio."

Sam became serious. "Peter, I've never let anyone into my studio. It's my sanctuary."

Peter looked at him intently. "Sam, we've been friends since childhood. If you don't trust me, who can you trust? I promise not to say a word to anyone."

After a moment of hesitation, Sam sighed. "Okay, Peter. You'll be the first to see my studio. But you must solemnly promise me that you won't tell anyone about it. Only under that condition will I take you with me."

Peter nodded eagerly. "I promise."

Back at Sam's loft, the two took an elevator to an underground floor that Peter had never noticed before. A long, dimly lit corridor led them to a large door. As the door opened, Peter entered the studio in awe and could hardly believe his eyes.

Right in front of them stood a TR-808, one of the oldest and most influential drum machines. "This device has shaped music more than any other," Sam explained. "Both hip-hop and techno owe their characteristic sound to the TR-808." Next to the TR-808 stood another legendary drum machine: the TR-909. "The TR-909 has also made music history. Its powerful kick drum sound and unmistakable hi-hats are heard in countless techno and house tracks."

Peter was impressed, but his attention was quickly drawn to another device—a large, elegant keyboard instrument. "Is that a Synclavier?" he asked incredulously.

Sam nodded. "Yes, and it's not just any Synclavier. This one once belonged to Michael Jackson. The new price of this instrument was about 180,000 euros. I was able to purchase it used from him at a more affordable price. It's an incredibly powerful tool that combines sampling and synthesis in a way that was far ahead of its time."

Peter continued through the studio and discovered a Minimoog. "Wow, a Minimoog!"

Sam smiled. "The Minimoog is a real gem. It was one of the first portable synthesizers and revolutionized the music industry. Artists like Kraftwerk, Gary Numan, and even bands like Pink Floyd used it to create iconic sounds. What makes it so special are its warm, powerful, yet versatile tones produced by analog oscillators. The Minimoog is simple to operate, but the sonic possibilities are virtually unlimited."

Peter gazed at the Minimoog in fascination. "I didn't know analog devices could have such an impact."

"Oh yes," Sam replied. "The analog circuits produce a natural, organic sound that digital devices often can't achieve. Every time I play the Minimoog, I feel a direct connection to the music. It's almost as if the instrument itself is alive and breathing."

Finally, Peter's gaze fell on an old, classic mixing console in the corner of the room. "And what about this mixing console?" he asked.

"That's a Neve 8078," Sam explained proudly. "It's one of the best analog mixing consoles ever built. Many of the greatest albums in music history were mixed on consoles like this. It has exceptional sound quality and offers warmth and depth that are often missing in digital consoles. Each channel has its own character, and the ability to fine-tune the sound makes it an indispensable tool in my studio."

Peter was overwhelmed by the collection and the history behind each device. "That really explains why your music sounds so unique. You rely on these incredible analog devices and create something that most people simply can't achieve with modern methods."

Sam nodded. "Exactly. It's the combination of human creativity and analog precision that makes my music so special. In a world that's increasingly relying on AI, I've decided to go back to the roots."

Peter looked at his friend with newfound admiration. "Thank you for showing me this, Sam. I promise to keep your secret."

The two friends left the studio and stood back in Sam's loft. Peter turned to Sam and said, "That was truly inspiring, Sam. I can't wait to get back to my own projects."

Sam smiled and placed a hand on Peter's shoulder. "Never forget, Peter, whatever you do…"

Peter completed the sentence with a smile: "Always stay creative."

Index

For Product Safety Concerns and Information please contact our EU representative GPSR@taylorandfrancis.com Taylor & Francis Verlag GmbH, Kaufingerstraße 24, 80331 München, Germany